Speech of the Right Rev. Dr. Hughes,
Delivered on the 16th, 17th and 21st Days' of
June, 1841. Being a Review and Refutation of
the Argument of Hiram Ketchum, Esq.,
Counsel for the Public School Society, Before
a Committee of the Senate of the State Of...

SPEECH

OF

THE RIGHT REV. DR. HUGHES,

DELIVERED

On the 16th, 17th and 21st days of June, 1841.

BEING

A REVIEW AND REFUTATION

OF

THE REMONSTRANCE OF THE PUBLIC SCHOOL SOCIETY,

AND

THE ARGUMENT OF HIRAM KETCHUM, Esq.,

THEIR COUNSEL,

BEFORE

A COMMITTEE OF THE SENATE OF THE STATE OF NEW YORK,

AGAINST

THE REPORT OF THE SECRETARY OF STATE

ON THE SUBJECT OF

COMMON SCHOOL EDUCATION.

———————

Specially Reported for the New York Freeman's Journal,

BY DR. J. A. HOUSTON.

———

NEW YORK:

PUBLISHED AT THE OFFICE OF THE FREEMAN'S JOURNAL,

150 FULTON STREET.

1841.

SPEECH

OF

THE RIGHT REV. DR. HUGHES,

DELIVERED

On the 16th, 17th and 21st days' of June, 1841.

BEING

A REVIEW AND REFUTATION

OF

THE ARGUMENT OF HIRAM KETCHUM, Esq.,

COUNSEL FOR THE PUBLIC SCHOOL SOCIETY,

BEFORE

A COMMITTEE OF THE SENATE OF THE STATE OF NEW YORK,

AGAINST

THE REPORT OF THE SECRETARY OF STATE

ON THE SUBJECT OF

COMMON SCHOOL EDUCATION.

———⟫◆⟪———

Specially Reported for the New York Freeman's Journal,

BY DR. J. A. HOUSTON.

———

NEW YORK:

PUBLISHED AT THE OFFICE OF THE NEW YORK FREEMAN'S JOURNAL.

NO. 150 FULTON STREET NEW YORK.

1841.

PREFACE

BY THE PUBLISHER.

IT has been thought advisable, for the information of those not con-versant with the history of the matter, to accompany the annexed Report of Bishop Hughes' late speech at Carroll Hall, with a brief statement of the course which the agitation of the question of Common School Education in the city of New-York, has taken during the past eighteen months.

Differing from the rest of the state, the city of New-York, or rather, the Common Council of that city, to whom a discretionary power on the subject was given by the Legislature, has for more than fifteen years past confided to a private corporation, styled "The Public School Society of New-York," almost the entire charge and business of Common School education; together with the management, disposition, and control of the public fund raised by taxation and otherwise for that purpose.

Much dissatisfaction had been felt with the system and the exclusive privileges of this society, especially among that portion of the community professing the Catholic faith, whose religious feelings and conscientious convictions were, not only not regarded, but violated, in so serious a manner by the teachings, and the irreligious or adverse influences brought to bear on the minds of the pupils, that they, almost without exception, withheld their children from the schools of the Society. In these circum-stances they established such free schools for the education of their children, as their limited means enabled them to provide; and they repeatedly petitioned the Common Council of the city, that a portion of the School Fund should be appropriated to the support of those schools, under such regulations as the Council might prescribe. The prayer of the petitioners was, however, invariably denied. But the petitioners still persevered.—Numerous and crowded public meetings were held on this subject in the city of New-York, during the past year, by those who were aggrieved, and who were interested in promoting the cause of uni-versal education. A determined spirit was manifested by all to effect a reform, and break down the monopoly, which secured the management of this most important interest of education in the hands of an irresponsible few. A petition for relief was again presented to the Common Council by the Catholics, and they prayed to be heard in its support before the Board, by counsel, or otherwise. The Public School Society remonstrated, and prayed to be heard in opposition. The 29th of last October was desig-nated by the Common Council for hearing the different parties on this subject; and on that day and the following one, a most important and highly interesting debate took place before the united Boards of Aldermen and Assistants. The Right Rev. Dr Hughes maintained the discussion on the part of the petitioners, and Hiram Ketchum and Theodore Sedgwick, Esqrs., spoke on the other side, as counsel for the Public School Society, assisted by several other gentlemen. The result, notwithstanding the clear and unanswerable reasoning of Bishop Hughes, was, as it had been on former occasions, adverse to the petitioners. Their application was denied.

Determined not to abandon what they considered to be a just and republican principle, the friends of freedom of education in the city of New-York, notwithstanding the adverse issue before the Common Council, prepared petitions, and forwarded them to the Legislature of the State, during its recent session at Albany, setting forth the grievances under which they laboured, and praying for redress The matter was referred by the Senate to the Hon John C. Spencer, Secretary of State and Superintendant of Common Schools, who made a report unfavorable to the present exclusive system, and distinguished alike by its clear and statesmanlike views, its liberal, just, and patriotic principles, and its unanswerable arguments—and in it he recommended that the system of Common School education prevailing throughout the state should be extended to the city of New-York.

The Public School Society, alarmed for the existence of their exclusive and unnatural prerogatives, sent a remonstrance to the legislature, against granting the petition of those who felt aggrieved by their system; and they also procured leave to be, and were, heard on the subject before a committee of the Senate, by their counsel, Hiram Ketchum, Esq. The petitioners were also heard at the same time before the same committee, by their counsel, James W. M'Keon, and Wright Hawkes, Esqrs. The committee subsequently reported a bill to the Senate, in conformity with the recommendation of the Secretary of State, which bill, after an animated debate, was postponed, by a vote of the Senate, to the second Tuesday of January next, by a majority of *one*. Many of the senators, however, who voted for the postponement, stated, that they did so, in order that they might have opportunity for obtaining more information on the subject, and not from any particular objection to the general features of the bill.

Mr. Ketchum's speech before the Committee, was elaborately reported, and published in the daily papers in the city of New-York, on or about the 10th of June instant, and the able speeches of Messrs M'Keon and Hawkes not having been reported, the Right Rev. Dr. Hughes undertook and delivered before a crowded and overflowing audience, on the evenings of the 16th, 17th, and 21st of June instant, a conclusive refutation of Mr. Ketchum's argument. The Bishop adopted this *viva voce* mode of review, in order to save the expenditure of time and labor, which would be necessarily attendant upon a written reply. The speech will, therefore, be found to exhibit all the freedom and freshness of an extemporaneous address; a circumstance which will not be found to detract in any manner from its force or interest.

The speech of Bishop Hughes was specially reported for the New-York Freeman's Journal, in the most full and accurate manner; and for greater convenience, and to preserve it in a more permanent shape, it is also published in the present pamphlet form.

New-York, June, 1841.

SPEECH

OF THE

RIGHT REVEREND DR. HUGHES,

ON THE SUBJECT

or

COMMON SCHOOL EDUCATION.

———

Public notice having been given in the daily papers of the city, that Bishop Hughes would, on the evening of Wednesday, the 16th of June, commence a Review and Refutation of the argument which was made by Hiram Ketchum, Esq., before a Committee of the Legislature, at Albany, in opposition to the Bill and Report of the Secretary of State, on the subject of Common School Education in the city of New York, a very large and respectable assemblage convened at half-past seven o'clock, on that evening, at Carroll Hall, to hear the address of the Bishop.

The Hon. Luther Bradish, Lieutenant-Governor, and several Senators of the State, who were then in attendance, in the city of New York, as members of the Court for the Correction of Errors, were amongst those present.

At the hour, specified in the notice, the meeting was organised by the appointment of Thomas O'Connor, Esq., as chairman, and Bernard O'Connor, Esq., Secretary.

RIGHT REV. BISHOP HUGHES then rose and spoke as follows:—

Mr. Chairman and Gentlemen, The subject of education is one which at this time agitates more or less every civilized nation. If we look across the ocean we find it the subject of discussion in France—in Prussia—in Holland—in Belgium—in Ireland—and even in Austria. It is not surprising, then, that this subject, which has but lately attracted the attention of governments, and of nations, should become one of deep and absorbing interest. But of all these nations there is, perhaps, not one which has placed education on that basis on which it is destined successfully, in the end, to repose.

In countries in which the inhabitants profess the same religion, whatever that religion may be, the subject is deprived of many of its difficulties. But in nations in which there is a variety of religious creeds, it has hitherto been found one of the most perplexing of all questions, to devise a system of education, which should meet the approbation of all. This subject has engaged the attention of our own government. In every State of the Union it has already been acted upon more or less fully. And in all these instances whether we regard Europe, or regard this country, we find that there is not a solitary instance in which religion, or religious instruction in a course of education, has been proscribed, with the exception of the city of New York. And this proscription of religion in this city is not an act of public authority. There is no statute authorising such an act; it has been the result rather of an erroneous construction put upon a statute, and which has been acquiesced in, rather than approved, for the last sixteen years. In the operation of that system, Catholics felt themselves virtually excluded from the benefits of education. Very shortly after that construction of the law was adopted, they felt themselves obliged to proceed in the best way that their poverty would allow for the education of their children. And whilst they have been taxed with the other citizens, up to the present hour they have received no benefit from the system supported by that taxation; but on the contrary, after having contributed what the law required, have been obliged to throw themselves back upon their own resources, and provide, as well as they might, the means of educating their children.

We have, from time to time, complained of this state of things. It has frequently been brought before the notice of the public. A Society—professedly the friend of education—having exercised supreme control over the whole question, we had no resource but to apply to that tribunal, which the law had authorised to use its discretion in distributing the money set apart for the purposes of education. We always insisted, in good faith, that the object—the benevolent object of this government was the education of the rising generation, and we never conceived that the question of religion, or no religion, had entered into the minds of those philanthropic public men who first established this system for the diffusion of knowledge. We applied, as I have remarked, at different times, to the tribunal to which allusion has been already made, and did so even till a very recent period, because before we could apply to the legislature of the State, it was requisite to comply with the forms prescribed, and that we should be first rejected by the Common Council of this city, to whom the State legislature had delegated the discretionary power to be exercised in the premises. That course was regarded necessary, and we adopted it. The result was as *we* anticipated—denial of our request—and then it was that we applied to the legislature of the State—submitted to them the grievances under which we labored, in the full confidence that there we should find a remedy.

Both before the Common Council and the Senate of this State, the means, which have been taken to defeat the proper consideration of our claims, have been such as we could not have anticipated in a country, where the rights of conscience are recognised as supreme. The test has been put, not as to whether we were proper subjects for education, but whether we were Catholics ¹ And in the course of the examination on which I am about to enter I shall have occasion to show, that from the beginning to the end, the one object of the members of the Public School Society has been to convince the public, that we were Catholics, and they, it would appear, calculate as the consequence, that if we were Catholics, then we had no right to obtain redress, or hope for justice.

In the course of my remarks, I shall be obliged to refer to distinctions in religion, the introduction of which into the discussion of this question, is ever to be much regretted; I shall have to speak of Catholics and of Protestants, and when I do so, let it be understood, that I do not volunteer in that, but the course pursued by that Public School Society, has imposed upon me the necessity to refer to these religious distinctions, and in doing so I trust I shall be found to speak of those who differ from me in matters of religion with becoming respect. I am not a man of narrow feelings— I am attached sincerely and conscientiously to the faith which I profess, but I judge no man for professing another. In the whole of my intercourse with Protestants, my conduct has been such they will be ready to acknowledge, in Philadelphia and elsewhere, that I am the last man to be accused of bigotry. But I feel that I should be unworthy of that estimation —that the denomination to which I belong would be unworthy of sustaining that position, which they are ambitious to occupy in the opinion of their fellow-citizens of other creeds, if they were to submit to the insult added to the injury inflicted on them by these men. I, for my own part, feel indignant at the recent attempt made to cast odium upon us, and our cause, and it is because that turns entirely on the question of religion, that I shall be obliged to speak of Catholics and of Protestants, and refer to those distinctions which should never have been introduced.

Before taking up the report of the Secretary of State, I shall refer briefly to the conclusion of the discussion before the Common Council. There we had, as you will recollect, legal gentlemen, and reverend gentlemen, advocates of the Public School Society, who had studied the question in all its bearings—volunteers and associates, and colleagues on the same side, and throughout that debate, the ground taken by them was, that if our petition were granted, favors would be conferred on us as a reli

gious denomination, tending to that against which all the friends
of liberty should guard—a union of church and state. So long
as that idea was honestly entertained by these gentlemen, I could
respect their zeal in opposing us. But that idea has disappeared, and yet their opposition has become more inveterate than
ever.

The very last sentence of the speech of Mr. Ketchum before
the Common Council of the City of New York, was a declaration
that this Society, so far from desiring a collision of this kind
with us, were men of peace, to whom even the moral friction of
the debate was quite a punishment—that for them it would be
a relief if our system of education were assimilated in its external aspect to that of the State. I will read his own words:—

Now, perhaps the gentleman may ask, if the system is to be changed, that we
should resort to the same course as is pursued in the country, where the people
elect their own commissioners and trustees But if we do, the schools must be
governed on the same principles as these, and the only difference will be in the
managers And if it is to come to that I am sure these Trustees will be very
willing, for it is to them a source of great vexation to be compelled to carry on
this controversy for such a period.

They are very unwilling to come here to meet their fellow-citizens in a somewhat hostile manner They have nothing to gain, for the society is no benefit to
them, and they give days and weeks of their time, without recompense, to the
discharge of the duties of their trust

I shall not now praise that Society. I have more than once
given my full assent to eulogiums on their zeal and assiduity ;
but Mr. Ketchum praises them and they praise themselves, and
at this period of the controversy they are entitled to no praise
from the thousands and thousands of the poor neglected children
of New York, whom their narrow and bigoted views have excluded from the benefits and blessings of education.

I shall now, before proceeding farther, take up the report of
the Secretary of State, and commence with that portion of it in
which he gives a brief sketch of the origin of this Society:—

"The Public School Society was originally incorporated in 1805, by chapter
108 of the laws of that session, which is entitled "An act to incorporate the
society instituted in the city of New York, for the establishment of a free school
for the education of poor children, who do not belong to, or are not provided for by
any religious society" In 1808 its name was altered to " The Free School Society
of New York ;" and its powers were extended " to all children who are the proper subjects of a gratuitous education " By chap. 25 of the laws of 1826 its name
was changed to "The Public School Society of New York," and the trustees
were authorised to provide for the education of all children of New York, not
otherwise provided for, " whether such children be or be not the proper subjects
of gratuitous education," and to require from those attending the schools, a mo
derate compensation , but no child to be refused admission on account of inability
to pay

" Thus by the joint operation of the acts amending the charter of the socie y,
of the statutes in relation to the distribution of the school moneys, and of the
ordinance of the Common Council, designating the schools of the society as the
principal recipients of those moneys, the control of the public education of the
city of New York, and the disbursement of nine-tenths of the public moneys
raised and apportioned for schools, were vested in this corporation. It is a per-
petual corporation, and there is no power reserved by the legislature, to repeal or

9

modify its charter. It consists of members who have contributed to the funds of the society, and according to the provisions of the last act, the payment of ten dollars constitutes the contributor a member for life. The members annually choose fifty trustees, who may add to their number fifty more."

He goes on to describe its different acts, by which its name and other attributes were changed, until from being a Society to take charge of the children that were not provided for by any religious society, they came to have the control of the whole system of education in New-York. The Report informs us, that the members of the Public School Society are so by virtue of a subscription of ten dollars—that they elect fifty trustees—that these fifty trustees have a right to appoint fifty others, and then the number is completed—that the City Council are members *ex-officio*, and this will, perhaps, go a great way in explaining the unwillingness of the Common Council to grant our petition.

The Society were so constituted, that when we went before the Common Council, we virtually went before a Committee of the Society.

In this state of things, the Governor of this State, with a patriotism and benevolence that entitle his name to the respect of every man that has regard for humane feeling and sound and liberal policy, declared for a system that would afford a good common education to every child. And though I have never before spoken in public the name of that distinguished officer of the State, I do now from my heart award to him my warmest thanks, and those of the community to which I belong, for the stand he has taken on this subject. An attempt has been made to victimize him because he favoured Catholics—he dared to manifest a humane and liberal feeling towards foreigners. He survived that shock however, and a recent excellent document from him, shewing that he is not any longer a candidate for public favour, authorizes me to say in this place, that every man who loves his country and the interests of his race, no matter what may be his politics, will cordially render the tribute of esteem and praise to that Governor Seward.

[The Chairman had, on taking his place, requested the meeting to refrain from interrupting the Right Rev'd. Speaker, or giving any demonstrations of applause, but here they could not restrain their feelings, and testified their concurrence in the sentiments of the Bishop in reference to Governor Seward, by a loud and enthusiastic burst of applause.]

Governor Seward knew too well,—Bishop Hughes continued,—the deep seated prejudices of a large portion of the community not to feel, that he had nothing to gain by being the advocate of justice to Catholics. But whatever may be that distinguished statesman's future history—whatever his situation—however much thwarted and opposed, and perchance for a moment partially defeated by those who call themselves the friends of education, it will be glory enough for him to have inscribed upon his monument, that whilst Governor of New-York, he wished to have every child of that noble State endowed and adorned in mind and intellect, and morals, with the blessings of education. (Renewed cheers.)

When, therefore, we presented, as every oppressed portion of the community has a right to do, our grievances to the honourable Legislature of the State, these gentlemen, who are represented by Mr. Ketchum through a speech of nine mortal columns—as the humble almoners of the public charity—these men who are burdened with their load of official duty,—which they are willing, Mr. Ketchum says, to put off—pursue us thither with unabated hostility. We supposed that the Public School Society would acquiesce in the justice of the plan of the Secretary. No! these humble men, all zeal for the cause of education, enter the halls of legislation with a determined spirit of opposition to us, which is, perhaps, unparallelled, considering the circumstances under which they acted.

One of the most difficult points in treating with these gentlemen, is to ascertain, in what particular situation, and under what particular circumstances, their responsibility may be discovered. They are, it is said, but agents, they are wealthy and powerful—have every advantage in opposing humble petitioners as we are, and with all these advantages they presented themselves there—not to dispute the justice of our claims, nor the correctness of the ground on which the honorable Secretary placed the question before the Senate,—but to appeal, even in the minds of Senators, to whatever they might find there of prejudice against the Catholic religion, and the foreigner and the descendants of the foreigner.

One of the documents of which they made use, was published in the "Journal of Commerce." This question had been in the Society made the special order of the day for, I think, Friday, the 20th of May. In the "Journal of Commerce" of the previous day, there was published a most calumnious article, full of all those traditions against our religion which the minds of the uneducated portion of some of those denominations inherit, and the Agent of the Public School Society sent, as we should understand, to represent justice and truth between citizens of the same country, is found distributing this paper all over the desks of the Senators! On that very day it was supposed that the vote on this very question would be taken, and the agent of the Public School Society is found supplying the Senators—for I have a copy of the papers thus furnished, with the member's name written at the top, and the article referred to marked with black lines, so that there could be no overlooking it—with an article containing a mock excommunication—a burlesque invented by Sterne, and inserted in his Tristram Shandy, but quoted by the Public School Society—for I hold it to be their act till they disclaim it—as a part of our creed, and made the ground of a sneer at the Secretary; "These are precious principles to be preserved in the consciences of your petitioners!" Religious prejudice will have its reign in the world. But it is a low feeling. Especially is it a low feeling in a country, in the fundamental principles of whose government and laws the great father of our liberties insisted, that conscience and religion should be ever free, and be regarded as above all law. There was to be no toleration, for that implied the power not to tolerate—the word was therefore excluded from the language of American Jurisprudence. And that being the case, it was painful to find an honorable body of men as the members of the Public School Society are regarded to be, employing such a means of approaching the Senate of New-York—that Senate to which Justice, if she found not a resting place upon the Globe, like the dove to the ark, might return, and expect every hand to be stretched out to receive her. (Loud applause.)

If they deny that they approached the Senate with that document— too vile and filthy to be read in this audience—but if any gentleman has the curiosity to see it, here (holding up a volume of Tristram Shandy,) here he may read it word for word—let them call their agent to account. We will not let them rob' us of our reputation. We stand ambitious to be considered worthy of membership in the great American family; let them not after depriving, us of the benefit of our taxes, destroy our reputation!

I will now, after this introduction, take up the remonstrance of the Society. It is impossible for me not to feel indignant when I think how these high-minded men have treated us, when I recollect how this same gentleman, who acted as their agent and distributed that calumnious paper, was once a candidate for office, and gladly received the signatures of Catholics. And this was the recompense he offered.

. I know not by whom this "Remonstrance" was drawn up. I know not whether all the members of the Board of Trustees approved of it; but if they did, I trust there were no Catholics present. In page 3, of this "Remonstrance," which is signed by the President, "Rob't. C. Cornell," we find the following declaration introductory to the subject :—

"The Legislature therefore, in 1813, when the first distribution was made, very naturally appropriated the amount apportioned to this city to these schools, in the ratio of the number of children taught in each This mode of distribution continued until 1824, when the subject was again brought before the Legislature by the jealousies, disputes, and difficulties, which had arisen among the recipients, and the conflicting parties presented themselves at Albany for the purpose of sustaining their respective claims "

Now, in all the foregoing applications — in all the Reports made by Committees of the Common Council, you will find, that there has not been one in which the subject of religion was not referred to as the *ground* of the refusal of our claims — in which it was not assumed, that the laws were opposed to giving education money — the Public School Fund, or any portion of it, to any religious denomination. This principle, it has been pretended, and the disputes among the sects, led to the alteration of the law in 1824. But if we refer back to the memorial proceeding from this Society itself, we will find, that no such thing existed at the time. We find, that Mr. Leonard Bleecker sent a memorial at that very period, 1824, in which he says.

"It will not be denied, in this enlightened age, that the education of the poor is enjoined by our holy religion, and is therefore, one of the duties of a Christian church Nor is there any impropriety in committing the school fund to the hands of a religious society, so long as they are confined in the appropriation of it, to an object not necessarily connected, or intermingled with the other concerns of the church, as for instance, to the payment of teachers, because the state is sure in this case, that the benefits of the fund, in the way it designed to confer them, will be reaped by the poor But the objection to the section, sought to be repelled, is, that the surplus monies, after the payment of teachers, is vested in the hands of , the trustees of a religious society, and mingled with its other funds, to be appropriated to the erection of buildings under the control of the trustees, which build, ings may, and in all probability will, be used for other purposes than school houses "

Here was the ground taken, and yet we hear these gentlemen before the Common Council say, it was on account of constitutional difficulties and religious differences; whereas, it was simply because the money had been used for an improper purpose.

In page 5 of this "Remonstrance," this Society takes the ground, in opposition to the view of its being a monopoly, and a close corporation, which it in fact is, that the same objection might be urged against hospitals, asylums for the blind, the insane, and the mute, dispensaries, and houses of refuge ; and they institute a comparison between these institutions and the public schools.

Now, as to the fact that the Public School Society is a close corporation, they themselves do not deny, that all citizens are excluded except those who can afford to pay $10 for membership.   They do not deny that, but justify it on the ground, that inasmuch as these are corporations for the management of such institutions as I have named, the same reason exists for the constitution of a corporation for the direction of the public schools.   And where then, pray, are the rights with which nature and nature's God have invested the parents of these children ? Pray, are they who are held competent to decide on the gravest questions affecting the interests of the nation, unworthy to have a voice in the education of their own children ?   And must they resign that to a corporation responsible neither to them nor to the public in any formal way ?   And, pray, are the people of New York lunatics, that they must have a corporation of keepers appointed over them ? If the doctrine of this " memorial" be correct, they are to be so considered. But there is this difference : they pay taxes for education, and they have a right to a voice and a vote in the manner in which their money is to be expended. If the people are to be treated as lunatics, mutes, or inmates of the House of Refuge, then the argument of the Public School Society is a good one.   I think the comparison instituted in the " Remonstrance" utterly fails.   I cannot dwell longer upon it.

I now come to a charge made against the petitioners :—

" At one time it was declared ' the public school system in the city of New York is entirely favorable to the Sectarianism of infidelity, and opposed only to that of positive Christianity ,' that ' it leaves the will of the pupil to riot in the fierceness of unrestrained lusts,' and is ' calculated to make bad and dangerous citizens ' "

Now, it is true, that we did view the Society as being opposed to religion.   There can be no doubt of that.   But if that be true, it is equally true, that the evidence on which we built that conclusion was furnished by themselves.   And how?   In every report of theirs it appears, that if any thing like a *religious* society presented itself, that character was enough to decide them in resisting its application.   You will find this evidenced in their vindication and defence, both by Mr. Sedgwick and Mr. Ketchum.   They contended that what *they* meant by religious instruction, was not religious instruction, and so it may be proper for me to enter a little into the examination of the meaning of these words.

When the Trustees make the religious character of a Society the ground of denying them a portion of their funds, what is it that constitutes the objection? They do not decide against the infidel, for it seems if the applicants had divested themselves of a religious character— if men of no religious profession, of no belief in a God or a future state, had presented themselves, no objection would be made, and on their own premises the Trustees would be obliged to concede to their request. What, then, was the reason of the refusal, except the *religious* character of the applicants? And had we not fair ground here for inferring, that they are opposed to religion? Examine their Reports. Here is one a Report of the Committee on Arts, Sciences, and Schools, of the Board of Assistants, on appropriating a portion of the School Money to *religious* societies for the support of schools. This is Document, No. 80, and at page 389 we read as follows:—

" The amount of one hundred and seven thousand dollars and upwards, as hereinbefore stated, has been raised by annual tax in this city, for purposes of a purely civil and secular character "

Well, if the education is to be purely "civil and secular," is religion mingled with it at all? And if religion is not to be mingled with it at all, then had we not a right to infer from their own document, that they were opposed to religion, and brought up the children without any knowledge of their responsibility to God, or of a future life, or of any of those great principles of religion on which the *very security* of society depends? Were we not justified in this inference? They refused our application, because we professed religion; and had we not a right to keep our children from the influence of a system of education that attempted to make a divorce between literature — that is, such literature as is suited for the infant mind—and religion, and to give instruction of a "*purely* civil and secular character," for which, we are told, $107,000 had been expended? How, I ask, can Mr. Cornell stand up and deny our charge, when such indisputable evidence of its truth is presented by *their own documents* ?

Did Mr. Cornell, when they defeated us, find fault with the Committee of the Assistant's Board, because they charged the Society with excluding religion from education? No! No! Enough it was, that religious societies should be defeated, and that they should continue to wield their complex monopoly. No matter that they were charged with having no religion—no matter at all, that their education was then described as "purely civil and secular."

This document goes on —

" The appropriation of any part of that sum to the support of schools *in which the religious tenets of any sect are taught to* ANY EXTENT"—

Well, if you excluded the tenets of all sects, you excluded *all* religion, because there is no religion except what is included in the tenets of sects. I defy you to teach the first principles of religion without teaching the tenets of sectarianism! Then it was, on the faith of their own documents, that we charged on them the character which they had assumed, on the strength of which they had successfully opposed, one after another, all the denominations who reverence religion.

The document proceeds —

—" would be a legal establishment of one denomination of religion over another; *would* conflict with all the principles and purposes of our free institutions, and *would* violate the very letter of that part of our constitution which so emphatically declares that ' The free exercise and enjoyment of religious profession and worship, without *discrimination or preference*, shall for ever be allowed in this state to all mankind.' By granting a portion of the School Fund to one sect *to the exclusion of others*, a ' preference' is at once created, a ' discrimination' is made, and the object of this great constitutional guarantee is defeated , taxes are imposed for the support of religion, and freedom of conscience, if not directly trammelled and confined, is not left in the perfect and unshackled state which our systems of government were intended to establish and perpetuate No difference can be perceived in principle between the taxing of the people of England for the support of a church establishment there, and the taxing of the people of New York for the support of schools in which the doctrines of religious denominations are taught."

And what are we to infer from this, except that they do not teach religion at all ? But they have changed their tactics. For they have, be it remembered, two strings to their bow — one for those who have religion, and one for those who have not, and so we actually find that whilst before the Common Council of New York they are destitute of religion, and give a "purely civil and secular education," at Albany they can be in favor of religion !

But there is still further evidence on this point. In page 18 of the Report of the Debate before the Common Council, we have the explanation of Mr. Ketchum, and it was one of the nicest managed points imaginable. Indeed, I could not but admire the sagacity of that gentleman and his associate, Mr. Sedgwick, in steering so adroitly between the teaching of religion and the not teaching of it, so that they· taught it, but yet you must not *call it* religion ' We put the gentlemen between the horns of a dilemma ; we said if you do not teach religion, then you are chargeable with making our common schools seminaries of infidelity , if you. do teach it, then you do exactly what you say excludes *religious* societies from a right to participate in the fund ! But these gentlemen, with great skill and critical acumen, and a little sophistry, were able to steer, by a line invisible to my mind, between the horns of the dilemma.

In describing the different kinds of instruction, Mr. Sedgwick says :—

" But, beyond that, there is still another branch of instruction which is properly called *religious*, and it is because those two phrases — ' religious' and ' moral' — have been used occasionally without an accurate apprehension of their signification, that the documents of the trustees have been misconstrued. But when the term ' moral' education is used, it only means that education which instructs the children in those fundamental tenets of duty which are the basis of all religion "

That is to say, you build the roof before you lay the foundation. For whence, I ask, will men get their knowledge of duty, if not based on a substratum of religion ? But here, morality, so called, is made the basis of religion. Well, let us apply this to the schools, and see whether any Christian parent would submit to have his children placed under such a system.

There is a child at one of these schools — they tell him not to lie, but children are inquisitive, and he asks, " Why should I not lie ?" You must answer, " because God abominates a lie" — there you teach religion ! You explain the reason why the child should not lie, that religion requires, and affords the reason of, the performance of the duty — not that the duty is the basis of religion. It is not enough to tell the child you are to speak the truth, and when you know and fulfil your duty, then you may learn, that there is a God to whom you are responsible. Washington himself, in his Farewell Address, cautioned the nation against the man who would attempt to teach morality without religion. (Cheers.) He says·

"Of all the dispositions and habits which lead to political prosperity, religion and morality are indispensable supports In vain would that man claim the tribute of patriotism, who should labor to subvert these great pillars of human happiness, these firmest props of the duties of men and citizens. The mere politician, equally with the pious man, ought to respect and to cherish them. A volume could not trace all their connexions with private and public felicity. Let it be simply asked, where is the security for property, for reputation, for life, if the sense of religious obligations DESERT the oaths, which are the instruments of investigation in courts of justice? And let us *with caution indulge the supposition*, that morality can be maintained without religion Whatever may he conceded to the influence of refined education on minds of peculiar structure, reason and experience both forbid us to expect, that national morality can prevail in exclusion of religious principle *"

Had we not, then, I would ask very respectfully, a right, when every petition had been rejected, on the ground, that the petitioners had a religious belief, to infer that religion formed no part of their system of education, and that the consequence, which we charged upon them, and that Mr. Cornell repudiated with so much horror, inevitably and justly followed; namely, that the Public School Society was favorable to the sectarianism of infidelity?

˙ I now go on to show what the Public School Society boast of having done in our regard. They had offered, in reply to our objections to passages in their books,—as, for instance, where it was stated that "John Huss was a zealous Reformer, but trusting to the *deceitful Catholics*, he was taken by them and burned at the stake,"—to expunge such objectionable passages when they were pointed out. ˙ They said, "Bishop, we submit our books to you, and if you will have the goodness to point out any objectionable passages, we will expunge them." Well, certainly there was something very plausible and apparently very liberal in this offer. But when the matter was pressed, it was found that all this was merely the expression of individuals—there was no *guarantee* that the books would be amended. Weeks, months might be spent in examining the books, and then the approbation of the Board was necessary in order to effect the alteration. Did they say that it should be given? Never.

˙ I pass now to another point; for observe, I do not at all think myself called on to say one word in vindication of the able, and eloquent, and satisfactory report of the Secretary of State (cheers). That is not necessary. The language of that document will be its own vindication when the petty sophistries raised against it shall have been long forgotten; for be assured, gentlemen, that whatever may be the temporary opposition to any public measure, from the moment that there is discovered to be inherent in it—of its essence—a principle of justice and equality, its ultimate triumph is certain, and all the opposition which it encounters will have no more effect on it than that of the breeze, which passes over the ocean—ruffling its surface, but destroying nothing of the mighty and majestic element which it seems to fret and disturb. (Cheers.)

˙ I take up this, then, not to vindicate the report, but rather in

16

reference to the insulting attempt, as 1 will call it, to deprive Catholics of the free exercise of their own consciences, and the respect and esteem of their fellow-citizens. In reasoning on the subject, observe the course that is taken by Mr. Cornell. He enters into a comparison between the schools of the Public School Society and ours—ours, supported in poverty, the humblest that may be, but still supported in a way sufficient to show our determination not to give up our rights, or relinquish the maintenance and defence of a sound and patriotic principle. But this gentleman compares these our schools with theirs—on which *more than a million of the public money has been expended,* whilst we have been virtually shut out from all benefit from the public funds, not by any law of the State, but by a vicious interpretation of the law. He requires us to furnish as perfect a system as they do with the expenditure of a million of dollars! He is reasoning with the Secretary, telling him, in effect, that we are troublesome and designing people, and he says:—

But having in view the stringency with which the same party insisted on the necessity of religious in juxtaposition with secular education, and the warmth with which they denounced the Public School system when they saw fit to charge it with excluding religion, and particularly when reference is had *to their avowed dogma, that there is no hope of salvation to those not of the Roman Catholic Church—which dogma is now taught in their schools.*

I thank God that the Catholics—the long-oppressed of three hundred years, during which the ear of the world was poisoned with calumnies against them—have now liberty of speech, and ability to exercise it, and I call Mr. Cornell to account for what he has here written, and to which he has affixed his name. He says:—

When reference is had to their avowed dogma, that there is no hope of salvation to those not of the Roman Catholic Church—which dogma is now taught in their schools.

The Catholics "avow" every dogma of their religion—but the two statements employed by Mr. Cornell are both *false.* It never was and never can be a dogma of ours, that there is "no hope of salvation to those not of the Roman Catholic Church." Neither is that dogma taught in our schools. This false statement must be accounted for by Mr. Cornell's ignorance of our doctrine on the one hand, and on the other, his disposition to injure us. I call upon him—I arraign him before the people of New-York, and the Senate whose confidence he has attempted to abuse, to prove his statement, or else to retract it.

And here it may be proper for me to *explain* something of this matter, for I know that in the minds of Protestants, almost universally, there is that idea; and that in the theological language of the Catholic Church there is apparent ground for entertaining it. But at the same time I do know, that that language, properly understood and fairly interpreted, does not imply the dogma imputed to us by Mr. Cornell.

It is very true that we believe, that out of the true Church of Christ there is no salvation—first proposition.

It is true that we believe the Catholic Church to be the true Church of Christ—second proposition.

It is very true that notwithstanding these propositions, there is no dogma of our creed which teaches that a Protestant may not hope to be saved, or may not go to heaven. Now how is this explained? In this way—When we speak of the Church, we mean the Church as Christ and his apostles did—in the sense, that the ordinary means for the salvation of mankind are the doctrines and institutions which Jesus left on earth, which have all descended in the Church with our history and our name. This we believe, but we do not believe, that God has deprived himself, because he instituted these things, of the means of saving whom he will. We do not believe that on this account the power of the Almighty is abridged. Hence it is consistent with our dogmas to believe that God, who is a *just* Judge, as well as a merciful Father, will not condemn any one for *involuntary* error. Their judgment will be individual; they were externally out of the Church, but was it by their own will, or the accident of their birth and education in a false religion? Did they believe that religion to be true in good faith, and in the simplicity of their hearts?—were they ready to receive the light and grace of truth as God might offer it to them? Then, in that case, though not belonging to the Catholic Church by *external profession*, they belonged to it by *their internal disposition.*

Consequently we are not authorised to deny hope of salvation to those not of the Catholic church, unless so far as the errors in which they have been involved have been voluntary and culpable on their part. And this is no new doctrine, as our opponents would have seen had they consulted the writings of the highest authorities in our church. St. Thomas Aquinas—one of the greatest minds that ever contributed to enlighten the human race, as Protestants themselves acknowledge—writing in the eleventh or twelfth century, speaks of a man who is not even a Protestant, but a pagan—a man who has never heard of Christ or of Christianity, and he, supposing that man to be moral—sincere—acting according to the best lights God has given him, tells us, God would sooner send an angel to guide him to the way of salvation than that *such* an one should perish. Such is the sentiment of St. Thomas Aquinas expressed in his works, and his works are approved of by our church. How then can Mr. Cornell, or any other individual say, that we enter into judgment respecting those who die out of the pale of our church? I publicly call upon Mr. Cornell to retract or qualify his official statement.

Sentiments according with these I have quoted from St. Thomas Aquinas, I have myself preached in the cathedral of New York, and similar ones have been abundantly proclaimed by others, and amongst them I would mention a very distinguished French bishop—then the Abbe Fressinous. In the third volume of his Conferences, he has one special sermon on the subject of exclusive salvation, and he shows that of all Christian denominations there is no one more abounding in charity on this point than the Catholic church. The same explanations are to be found in the writings of Bossuet, St. Francis of Sales, and St. Augustine.* With these facts well known how did

* SALVATION OUT OF THE CHURCH.—In concluding this simple and brief view

3

those gentlemen venture to take advantage of their, and our relative situations, and calumniate us when we had no opportunity of repelling the unfair attack?

Besides, Mr. Cornell says,—"which is now taught in their schools." I deny the truth of that statement, and demand his authority.

But now, would it, think you, be improper on my part, considering that Mr. Cornell is not present, to imitate some of the liberties which he has taken with us in our absence?

Throughout this document he has labored to prove, that we are Catholics, and not only that, but to show what our religion is, though I am rather at a loss to imagine where he studied Catholic theology, in which if he should persevere, I would suggest to him to consult better authorities than the "Journal of Commerce," and "Tristram Shandy." (Laughter and cheers.)

Now, it never occurred to us to ask of what religion is Mr. Cornell, and the Public School Society. The whole ground assumed by them is, that they are *not* a "religious society"—well, what are they? Are they an irreligious society? Not at all. They are members of churches; and I have taken the pains to ascertain that Mr. Cornell is a member of Dr. Spring's church, and if he lectures the Catholics would it be very wrong in me to speak of the doctrines of *his* creed? Let us look at the Westminster Confession of Faith, the rule of Presbyterian dogma, and see whether Mr. Cornell opens the gates of Heaven to all religious denominations. I quote from the Westminster Confession as adopted and amended in the United States, and published by Towar and Hogan, Philadelphia, in 1827. In page 111 it is said—

"The visible church consists of all those throughout the world who PROFESS the true religion."

—So to be a member of the visible church you must "profess" the true faith—"together with their children"—happy children! (A laugh.) —"and this is the kingdom of our Lord Jesus Christ, the house and

---

of the Catholic doctrine, it may be well to state here what is to be correctly understood, of that Catholic sentiment, "OUT OF THE CHURCH THERE IS NO SALVATION"

"We do not pretend to deny, (says Mr Beigier,) that there are numbers of men born in heresy who by reason of their little light, are in *invincible* ignorance, and consequently excusable before God · these, in the opinion of all judicious, Divines, ought not to be ranked with heretics." This is the very doctrine of St. Augustine, (Epis 43, ad gloriam et alias n 1.) St. Paul tells us, in his Epistle to Titus, c. 3, 'A man that is a heretic, after the first and second admonition, avoid, knowing that he that is such a one, is subverted and sinneth, being condemned by his own judgment.' As to those who defend an opinion, either false or perverse, without obstinacy, and who have not invented it from a daring presumption, but received it from their parents after they were seduced and had fallen into error, if they diligently and industriously seek for the truth, and if they hold themselves ready to embrace it as soon as they shall have found it, such as these also are not to be classed with heretics" L 1, de Bapt. contra Donat. c. 4, n. 5.

"Those who fall with heretics, without knowing it, believing it to be the church of Jesus Christ, are in a different case from those who know that the Catholic church is spread over the whole whole world." L 4, c. 1, n. 1.

"The church of Jesus Christ may have through the power of her spouse, children and servants; if they grow not proud, they shall have part in his inheritance; but if they are proud, they shall remain without." Ibid. c. 16, n. 23.

family of God, OUT OF WHICH THERE IS NO ORDINARY POSSIBILITY
OF SALVATION."

Here is another statement of Mr. Cornell.—

" They are not merely the incidental remarks of the historian, or extracts from
the Holy Scriptures ' without note or comment,' to which such strong exception
has been taken in relation to the public schools, but they are such as ever have,
and in the opinion of your remonstrants, must ever tend, if sustained *by tax imposed upon the anathematized* portion of the community, to destroy public harmony ;
and such as would prove any thing rather than a ' social benefit.' "

Now by using the word "anathematized " he conveys the impression that all out of the pale of our church are under our anathema. I
demand the proof. I have studied our holy religion many a day, but
never yet have I discovered any such anathema, and I defy Mr. Cornell to point it out.

Mr. Cornell goes on to say —

" Your remonstrants had supposed that the fact of the Public School Society
being composed of men professing every variety of religious faith would *neutralize sectarian tendencies and secure* it against abuse "

Now, there is something exceedingly specious in this, but it is
indeed a very spurious position. They refuse our application on
the ground that we are a religious society, and when we then
charge them with not being a religious society, they repudiate it
as a stigma on their character. And what is their remedy?
That they " will neutralize sectarian tendencies by the variety of
the religions that they introduce." How is this? They are all
members of Churches—and that does them honor—but whenever
they come within the magical circle of their official character,
then, like negative and positive brought together in just propor-
tions, they neutralize each other'! Is this really the position
that these gentlemen assume? How are the Trustees chosen ?
In the most beautiful manner ? One or two Catholics are taken—
a Universalist—perchance, and so of other denominations, and
then they say " we are of all religions !" You will find that the
mass of the Society belong to one sect, of which little or nothing
is said, and that an odd one is taken from each of the other sects
to sanctify their acts! There is a sufficient majority of one
denomination. There is a tendency and aim which I am not
unwilling to proclaim—a secret understanding—not so very
secret either—to the effect that "as there is a large foreign
population in New-York, and mostly Catholic, our liberties
would not be safe unless the interests of Catholics, were not
neutralized in their education." We reject that idea with scorn,
that Catholics have to learn the principles of liberty from them.
At a period when Protestantism was as little dreamed of
as steam navigation, Catholics were the schoolmasters to the
nations of the world, in the principles of liberty. They were
Catholics who wrung the great charter of English liberty from
the hands of the tyrant. And was that their first effort in the
cause of freedom ? No. That was only the written recognition
of their rights, which the encroachments of his predecessors
had diminished, and having thus secured their rights, they maintained them down to the period of the Reformation, when their

4

high and honorable notions of liberty were trampled in the dust, and were never restored till the Revolution; and when that so boasted event in the history of England took place, it only recognized the rights lost at the period of the Reformation, which Catholics for centuries before had known and enjoyed. Let them not say then that our religion is inimical to liberty. That is a reproach which we spurn—which we abominate and abhor! We have nothing to learn from them of human liberty. Their part is to imitate us, not ours to imitate them! (Loud applause.)

If that is the principle referred to, we understood it perfectly well, and it is of no use for these gentlemen to moot it for the purpose of shewing that our claim should be denied. Was that, indeed, their object? Not at all. But their object was, with hands that should have been better employed, to rake up that wretched remnant of prejudice against us, and pander to the vitiated taste that could relish it.

We see, then, that so far as this "Remonstrance" is concerned, there is not one solitary proposition which should for one moment have arrested the mind of the Legislature. The Bill proposed by the honorable Secretary of State, contemplated no special favour. Much as I honor that distinguished individual, I would not esteem him as I do if he had in his Bill proposed anything which should have raised us above our fellow-citizens of other denominations. But the Bill only places us on an equality with others—with that we are satisfied—with nothing less will we ever be satisfied. (Loud cheers.)

But hitherto these gentlemen have assumed various shapes. They have viewed with self-complacency the beauty of their system, and as for their few schools—few in comparison with the number of destitute and unprovided children—I have nothing to say against them. I proposed to place our schools under their direction, so far as regarded their police and management. But I would not permit them to teach our children that Catholics were deceitful—that Galileo was put into the Inquisition and punished for the heresy that the earth revolved on its own axis around the sun. That and similar statements of partizan writers, long and generally believed, begin to be better understood. Behind the Anti-Catholic credulity in which they have hitherto been entrenched, there is now going on a deeper and sounder spirit of criticism, conducted by eminent Protestant as well as Catholic writers. At the very time of his trial, his doctrine was held and avowed by eminent Cardinals, and the Pope himself declared that as a philosophical proposition, it was no heresy. His case is entirely misunderstood.

Galileo's crime was not teaching sound philosophy, but bad theology—wishing the Church to declare that his theory was in accordance with the Scriptures. For reasons like this I would not allow them to mislead our children. But was willing to allow the gentlemen the external management of our schools. They, however, would have *universal rule*, or none at all.

What has been their panacea for all complaints? To invite the

City Council to visit the Schools! And certainly, I presume, it would be impossible to visit their Schools without being satisfied with their *appearance*. But had I been able to have made my voice heard in the Senate of the State, when they made the proposition to visit their schools, I should have proposed something like an amendment. I would have prayed these Senators, in the name of humanity and their country, of all the benevolence that beats in the human breast, to visit—not the schools—but the lanes and alleys, and obscure resorts of the poor neglected children of New-York, and there see, not how much is done, but how much is left undone. These are the portions of the city that should be visited. It is utterly impossible, owing to their scattered condition, to learn the numbers of children in this city who are deprived by these gentlemen of the blessings of education. We who mingle with the people and have the opportunity of learning their dislike of this system—that they would no more trust their children to it, than to that tyrannical system of British mis-government which their fathers knew so well, and from which they derived the sad legacy of ignorance and poverty. I refer to the laws which made education a crime in Ireland, and which have left the inhabitants of that country the degraded, but unbroken people that they are this day, after a persecution of near three hundred years. (Cheers.)

It is for these poor, neglected, uneducated children, that I plead. Their parents will not send them to the Public School whilst constituted as at present, and I approve of their resolution. I trust that they never will send their children to schools managed by men who can send to the Senate of this State a burlesque upon our creed, and represent it as a genuine exhibition of our faith and principles. Rather will we trust to the kind and merciful Providence of God, than voluntarily relinquish a principle by which we maintain the right implanted in the breast of every parent and secured by the laws, to have a voice in the education of his child. It is these children that should be visited. Then would these honorable Senators, whom I know to be above all these petty prejudices which have been appealed to, do justice, and apply a remedy so far as the law would authorize them.

I must now soon conclude my remarks for this evening. I will merely refer to the objection of the Society to the Bill of Mr. Spencer — its tendency to introduce party politics. Every thing is held in this country to be in the hands of the people, yet these gentlemen, after enjoying a monopoly for sixteen years, think it a great misfortune if the tax-payers should be allowed a voice at all in the selection of the teachers in the schools which they support, or any share whatever in their management.

The next objection to the Bill, is its want of uniformity. Because they happen to have school-houses exactly one like the other, and have a uniform style of books, the large and liberal, and statesmanlike plan of the honorable Secretary, should be given up because, forsooth, these "humble almoners" pronounce it void of uniformity! "Humble almoners," who after coiling their roots around the Common Council, and making them judges in the cause, go to Albany to defeat our claims. Well, they may call themselves "humble almoners" if they please, but they remind me very much of the beggar in Gil Blas, who when he asked alms always took good care to have his musket ready!

I have now gone briefly through this part of the subject, and I ask you whether we can have any confidence in men who can stoop to such artifices as I have exposed? I call upon them to vindicate themselves from the dishonor of having circulated that document from Tristram Shandy. It was done by one of their colleagues and their official agent, who when charged with it, replied that he had done so under instructions. What instructions? Did they instruct him? If not, let them say so by a public act. Until they do so, we justly charge them with being the traducers of our reputation. I charge them on the ground that they are responsible for the act of their agent: and they should have known better. Gentlemen claiming to be exclusively the judges of what is a proper system of education—who held that you are unworthy of having any thing to do with the schools of New York—should have known that that document was from Tristram Shandy, written, I presume, for his amusement, by Mr. Sterne—who though numbered amongst the clergy of the Church of England, was believed to be an infidel—a man who secretly scoffed at every thing sacred—and the working of whose rank imagination is too offensive for the eye of delicacy. Surely, then, these gentlemen should not have drawn weapons from such a source for the purpose of destroying the reputation of any class of their fellow-citizens.

This is not the first occasion on which we have been misrepresented, and religious gentlemen whose avowed purpose it is to preach the gospel of peace, have taken up the habit of abusing us, and have rung the changes on this topic, till in some instances some of their audiences, more liberal than they, have left the place disgusted. They remind me of a saying of this same Sterne, who when quizzing the credulity of the people of England—for he was a great wag—said that occasionally he was straitened for the price of a dinner, but he could always manage to make a good meal of *Cheshire cheese*; but it also happened, that oftentimes he was in a similar strait in his official capacity, and was called on to preach when he had not a word of a sermon prepared, and then he took "a fling at Popery." The people went away edified and delighted. For this reason, he says, I call *Popery* my "Cheshire cheese!" (Loud laughter.) It seems to me that the occupants of half the pulpits of New York are nearly in the same predicament, and would die of inanimation, were it not that their stock of "Cheshire cheese" is still unexhausted. (Renewed laughter and applause.)

I think I can safely say, that in none of our churches will you hear such abuse. We never touch upon secular affairs; you will not even hear from our pulpits harangues about abolition. We explain and defend our creed, and, I trust, preach charity and peace and order. But it is not so with those who assail us as I have described, as I will have occasion to show when treating of Mr. Ketchum's speech, which I intend to do on to-morrow evening.

The Bishop then concluded, after speaking nearly two hours, and a vote of thanks having been passed to the Chairman, the large and attentive meeting adjourned.

THURSDAY EVENING.

The audience on this occasion was still more numerous than on the previous evening. Several distinguished Senators, and influential gentlemen of other denominations, were present. The meeting was organized by the appointment of the same Chairman who presided at the former meeting, and at 8 o'clock the Right Rev. Bishop HUGHES resumed his remarks as follows —

The question, gentlemen, which has called us together has had two stages of progress, which must be kept distinct in order to comprehend its present position. We have from time to time applied to the Common Council of this city for relief, which we knew they had the power to grant; and we had applied, as it were, in an isolated, and, if you please, as to appearance, in a somewhat sectarian character. The reasons of this will be easily understood, when you reflect that we had no intention to disturb the system of education so generally approved by our fellow-citizens. Our object was not to destroy that which was good for *others*, if they thought it so, but to find something that might be equally good for ourselves. Accordingly we applied as Catholics, because it appeared that there were no other denominations whose consciences suffered under the operation of that system. And we did suppose, that these considerations would have had some weight with the honorable Council. We might—as we are reproached with not having done—we might have interfered with the regulations of these schools—asked for a different order of books—required the erasure of such and such passages, and the insertion of others. They reproach us with not doing so; but if we had done so, it would, in the first place, have been pains thrown away, and in the second place, we might thereby have disobliged many of our fellow-citizens of other denominations. Without our at all pressing the question upon them farther than observing, that even the reading of the Holy Scriptures, according to the Protestant version, was looked upon by us as an invasion of our conscientious rights, they took it up as an objection against the reading of the Scriptures at all, as if the presence of a Bible within the walls of a school was a thing we could not bear. It is needless to say how wrong that inference was; but we did not at all wish to disturb the Protestant's approbation of *his* version of the sacred volume, nor the order that seemed so generally approved, and that was the reason of the mode of our application.

In the course of my speech therefore, you will understand that we did not so apply for relief because we wished to be apart, separate from the rest of the community—that it was not because we were exclusive, or intolerant, as they have charged upon us; but because we supposed that they would not wish to have their children hear the Catholic version of the Bible read; and, therefore, they had *no right* to impose on our children the hearing of the Protestant version. If that be sectarianism, then we plead guilty to the charge, but without feeling and acting so, we could not have our consciences simple, and in their integrity, upright towards God.

When, however, after having gone through the ceremony—for it was nothing else—of appearing before the Common Council, and having been heard and denied, as a matter of course, when we had gone through this ceremony required by the formulary of the law, then indeed we threw ourselves on our general rights as citizens, and appealed to that tribunal to which we must always look with confidence for the redress of every grievance that presses on us in our social condition. Nevertheless, our opponents followed us there, and fastened upon us the character, in which it had been the duty imposed on us by necessity, to appear before the Common Council.

We have had occasion already to point out some evidences of the use made of that in the "Remonstrance." You saw with what recklessness of truth—I am sorry to say—it was charged in that document, that we were intolerant—that we taught there was no salvation out of the Catholic church, and so forth. There are in that document of the Public School Society many other passages requiring examination, but as the substance of them is contained in the speech of the learned gentleman, who was their official organ before the Senate, I suppose that the refutation of the one will be the refutation of both, and therefore I deem it unnecessary to refer farther to that memorial.

They—that gentleman particularly—referred in the course of the debate to a proposition for accommodation, which was made on the part of the Society previous to the last decision of the public Council. They alleged that nothing could be fairer ; but when we had examined that, we found that of not a solitary grievance of which we had complained did it take notice—not the slightest notice. The whole proposal was, that they should correct the books, so far their guardianship of the rights of conscience—for they are conscience keepers for the several sects in this community!—would allow. They would accommodate us by striking out passages insulting and offensive to our minds, and injurious to our children. That was all the amount of the concession. Then the second proposition was, that they would purchase from us—they can afford to do so—the only schoolhouse which our humble means have enabled us to erect during the sixteen years of privation from the benefits of Common School Education. These were the only two features that distinguished that offer of accommodation. But Mr. Ketchum did not find it convenient to read the propositions that we submitted at the same time, and which, candor should have acknowledged, removed from us every imputation of being actuated by sectarian motives, or having in view the appropriation of the public money to the propagation of our religion.

I will now commence with the reading but a small portion of that, sufficient however to show you that on this ground, so far as information was concerned they had it, and if with that in their possession they concealed the truth, and suppressed it, on their heads be the responsibility that attaches to such conduct.

What is the great difficulty—the legal difficulty? That public money cannot be applied to sectarian uses. Very well. We met that ; we said here are propositions that cover our whole ground —

"That there shall be reserved to the Managers or Trustees of these schools respectively, the designation of the teachers to be appointed, who shall be subjected to the examination of a Committee of the Public School Society, shall be fully qualified for the duties of their appointment, and of unexceptionable moral character; or in the event of the Trustees or Managers failing to present individuals for these situations of that description, then individuals having like qualificatilons of unexceptionable character, to be selected and appointed by the Public School Society, who shall be acceptable to the Managers or Trustees of the Schools to which they shall be appointed, but no person to be continued as a teacher in either of the schools referred to against the wishes of the Managers or Trustees thereof."

That was the first proposition, showing them, that so far as the teachers were concerned, all we wanted was men in whom we could place confidence. The second proposition was :—

"2d. That the school shall be open at all times to the inspection of any authorized agent or officer of the city or State government, with liberty to visit the same, and examine the books used therein, or the teachers, touching the course and system of instruction pursued in the schools, or in relation to any matter connected therewith."

So that there was no concealment there, they themselves should be the inspectors, and I will say it boldly, that if they had been actuated by that deep feeling of humani y for which they claimed credit, they would have accepted that proposal to take our children under their care, affording to them the same means of gaining future happiness as they did to others.

The document goes on :—

"The undersigned are willing that, in the superintendence of their schools, every specified requirement of any and every law passed by the Legislature of the Sta e, or the ordinances of the Common Council, to guard against abuse in the matter of common school education, shall be rigidly enforced and exacted by the competent public authorities.

"They believe that the benevolent object of every such law is to bring the means of education within the reach of the child of every poor man, without damaging their religion, whatever it may be, or the religious rights of any such child or parent.

"It is in consequence of what they consider the damag ng of their religion and their religious rights, in the schools of the Public School Society, that they have been obliged to withdraw their children from them. The facts which they have already submitted, and which have been more than sustained by the sentiments uttered on behalf of the society, in the late discussion, prove that they were not mistaken.

"As regards the organization of their schools, they are willing that they should be under the same police and regulations as those of the Public School Society. The same hours, the same order, the same exercises, even the same inspection.

"But the books to be used for exercises in learning to read or spell, in history, geography, and all such elementary knowledge, as could have a tendency to operate on their hearts and minds, in reference to their religion, must be, so far as Catholic children are concerned, and no farther, such as they shall judge proper to put in their hands. But none of their dogmas, nothing against the creed of any other denomination shall be introduced."

Reference is here made to the sentiments uttered by the advocates of the Public School Society, in their opposition to our claims before the Common Council. Many of my present audience were perhaps there, and they can remember what an array of individuals, otherwise distinguishèd by their character—what an array of bigotry and prejudice—and we must say—of profound ignorance, was presented against us. One reverend gentleman came there and said in reference to our objection respecting the *Protestant version* of the bible, that one of our comments taught " the lawfulness of murdering heretics." Before the Common Council, I brought that gentleman to account, and I assure you, that considering his grey hairs and the respect that is due to age and the sacred character of a minister of peace, I felt humbled at beholding the degraded position in which he found himself before I had done. He had, however, obtained a copy of an old version of the scriptures, published by the Catholic refugees in the time of Queen Elizabeth, who wishing to prepare the way for an invasion, by the Spanish, wrote a series of notes on the scriptures, which they thought would tend to effect that end. So soon, however, as these notes became known in England and Ireland, they were scouted with horror by all professing the Catholic name. A few copies of that version, however, remained lost and forgotten, and an ignorant publisher in Cork, thinking to make a profitable speculation, obtained one of them, and not knowing;—as was afterwards proved,—the difference between it and the authorised version, he undertook to publish another edition of it. In the process of publication, however, the character of the work became known, and the Arch-Bishop of Dublin, forbade the publication. The publisher was ruined, and he commenced a suit, for damages. The matter was referred to in Committees of the House of Commons, and of the House of Lords, and to all the particulars of the case was, of course, thus given the greatest possible publicity. Well, the publisher being deprived of his anticipated sale in Ireland, where the Catholics would not purchase such a book, thought that by sending some to this country, people as ignorant as himself, might purchase them, and thus the work might not prove a dead loss. In this way, a copy fell into the hands of one of these gentlemen, and what did they do? Why, about the very same period that " Maria Monk" was published,—and I know not but from the same press,—they emitted an edition of this bible, in order to excite public odium against their Catholic fellow-citizens! It was then, with a copy of that in his hand, that that clergyman came forward to prove, by means of that forgery, that we taught the lawfulness of murdering heretics. Then, besides that, there was another gentleman, and he, in speaking on the subject of these very schools, and offering reasons why we should be denied the benefits of education, instituted a comparison—all the others had with great *professions* of respect and benevolent feeling for us, said " it was not because we were Catholics," that they opposed us, oh! no, they always qualified it—but he instituted a comparison between the religion of Fenelon and Voltaire, and with marvellous candor, forgetting the preface, admitted that he opposed us because we were Catholics! This gentleman said, that if he had no alternative he would sooner be of the religion of Voltaire, than of that of Fenelon. These are the sentiments to which I allude, and to which reference is here made when we say that such sentiments are only calculated to strengthen the conviction that our Catholic children, from the prejudices against their parentage and religion, had no chance of justice in those schools. The Committee to whom was referred an examination of the schools, make a report, and in that, after quoting the two propositions, for an accommodation, they take occasion to say :—

"Your Committee deem it proper to remark, in vindication of the School Society, that they were only one of the numerous remonstrants against the prayer of the petitioners. Their views were represented at the late discussion before the Board only by their legal advisers, Messrs. Sedgwick and Ketchum. The other gentlemen who participated in the discussion represented other bodies, which are not in any manner connected with them. Sentiments were uttered by them which the School Society do not entertain, and for which they are not justly accountable."

So they say, but by whom? It would go abroad that this was a declaration from the whole body of the Public School Society. I do not believe that was the fact, and I have no reason to believe it. Because I do know that these gentlemen *used*, or at least *admitted* this sentiment—this bad sentiment of their associates—for the purpose of defeating us, and they were perfectly satisfied with the victory, without at all disclaiming the dishonorable means they had employed to secure it. But as easily could the English efface the stigma that rests upon them from their employment of the Indian's tomahawk during their warfare with America.

And I ask them, is there on their records a disapproval of the declaration of Dr. Spring, or of Dr. Bond? The one that we would murder heretics, and the other, that the religion of Voltaire was to be preferred to that of Fenelon? Have they in any one official document disavowed that? We challenge them to show that the question of a disclaimer has ever been mooted. On the contrary, we have reason to believe that they approved of these statements made by Drs. Spring and Bond, and that from their own document too, signed by their President and Secretary, which goes nearly as far. And yet these are the men to whom we are required to give the management of the education of our children! They have hedged education around with an impenetrable wall, beyond which no applicant from our body can be admitted, except on terms that violate our civil and religious rights. A state of ignorance and degradation is the destiny assigned to those who will not submit to their Procrustean system, to the dimensions of which all must submit to be adapted.

The Society acknowledge that Messrs. Ketchum and Sedgwick are their official organs. Well, we find Mr. Sedgwick, in the speech referred to, on last evening, absolutely disclaiming the teaching of religion. He said it was a mistake to suppose that what was called religious instruction, meant any thing more than simple morality, which he stated to be the basis of all religion. And do these gentlemen intend to reverse the order of the Almighty, and, by giving this precedence to morality, to say that men must be good without a motive, and then they may learn religion? How then can they quarrel with us for saying that they attempted, what Mr. Spencer says well, is impossible, to *divorce* religion from education? It was on that ground that they appeared before the Common Council and defeated our claim; for as you saw yesterday, and see to-day—the crime charged upon us—the disqualifying circumstance, was that we belonged to a religious society, and the public money was, not to be appropriated in any way, except in the promotion of a "purely civil and secular education." When we told them that we supposed they were sincere in their declarations, and that by divorcing religion from education, thus leaving the children without the necessary motive to virtue and morality, and wholly destitute of any principle, to curb their rising passions, they seemed to exclaim "Oh! what an impious set of men you suppose us to be, Atheists!" No, not exactly, but I accuse you of being what you, yourselves, assume. You defeat all applications made by applicants professing religion. You contend that religion must not be any part of State education. Well, then, how can you be dissatisfied, if we call you anti-religious according to the principles you have, yourselves, assumed?

The fact is that in order to conciliate those whose minds are haunted by a certain spectre of a union between Church and State, and in order to bring them to the support of the Society, they pretended to meet their views exactly, and then again on the other hand, attempted to satisfy the scruples of conscientious parents by playing the several sects one against the other, and with so much adroitness, that the whole community came to the desired conclusion that the interests of education and morality were perfectly safe in the hands of the Society, and could not be safe in the hands of any other.

In taking up the speech of Mr. Ketchum, I must premise that he has divided it into two parts, and that of the many columns by which it is supported, the first two or three are occupied with a detailed *history* of the legislatlio, so called, of the Common Council, on this question. Now, I understand the part of this gentleman—who has perhaps as deep a knowledge of the mystery of political wire-drawing as any other gentleman of his profession in the State—I understand his introduction of this matter, entirely foreign to the subject. His object was to impress the mind of the Senators with the idea that in New York, the question had been decided—that Board of Aldermen had been changed—the position of parties changed—applications had been made from time to time, for sixteen years, and that after the gravest reflection, under all possible variety of circumstances, the answer uniformly was, that it would be a violation of something that he calls "*a great principle,*"—which however, he does not think proper to define—if our claim were admitted. He wished to convey the idea that if there had been any thing just, or proper, or true, in our claims, it could not have escaped the notice of public officers in New York—the immediate representatives of the people, and that consequently the Senators should approach the subject with minds already biassed and prejudiced against us. The gentleman wished to lead the honorable legislators to say "What! shall we on the examination of one hour—at this distance from the city of New York—undertake to reverse the judgment sustained by the uniform, concurrence of the various Boards that have constituted the public councils of that city for sixteen years!"

There was great *generalship* in all that on the part of the learned gentleman.

But I dispute the principle *in toto*, which the gentleman assumes, and before that honorable Senate I would maintain, that the gentleman has no foundation whatever for his assumption ; and that this question should be viewed by them, as if approached for the first time.

And what is my reason for assuming this position? You will mark that the learned gentleman, frequently styles the Common Council "the representatives of the people," my argument, in reply, then is, that so far as regards this School question they never were the "representatives of the people," for that question never was made one that could affect their election in the most remote degree. At least, so we thought. So far as we are concerned, we are right. True, whilst we were meeting to study this subject, and bring it under public notice, these gentlemen of the Society were ever and anon charging us with political designs, and I recollect something of an amusing nature connected with that. It was my duty, in the day succeeding the debate, before the Common Council, to proceed to Albany for the purpose of giving Confirmation—I went—preached on three times next day, Sunday,—on Monday, I drove to Troy, for the purpose of visiting the churches there, and on Tuesday, I returned to this city. Well, what was the story,—of course I do not say got up by these gentlemen, nor by the Public School Society—but it was said, that I, having taken tea with the Aldermen, a bargain was struck between us, and I was to go to Albany, to get the Catholics to vote against the Governor, and then all would be right! (Laughter.) That was a specimen of the stories that were circulated ; but while we were thus charged, they who brought the accusation, were themselves not idle in that very department. The subject was introduced to their pulpits, and their congregations were lectured on it, and from that may be traced the attempt to defeat Governor Seward.

But we never made this a political question, and the Common Council have never acted on it "as the representatives of the people," because it never was applied as a test ;—but if the question were put between the Secretary's plan, and the Public School Society, the latter would soon break down any Board that would undertake to support them. (Cheers.)

We were denied, it is true, by the Common Council, but we never looked on them as acting in that matter, as the representatives of the people. We regarded them as independent judges. And really there is little ground for surprise at their decisions in the premises.

Now I will suppose a case. Let us take that of a bank, for it is perhaps as good an illustration as I can furnish at the moment. A citizen has a controversy with the bank, and that controversy comes to a trial. The citizen complains that he is injured by the directors of the bank, he makes out his case, but in the end, he finds, contrary to all his just anticipations, and all his views of justice, that he is defeated, and judgment given against him. Well, he thinks this very hard. But he happens to learn that the *judge* before whom the case was tried, and the jury who rendered the verdict, are all directors of the bank!—and his wonder at the result of the trial ceases. Do you see the application? These gentlemen after having excluded all religious societies—made the word religion a kind of disqualification in a Christian community, in the year 1824; after that with the subtlety, which proves that they are wise in their generation, they got an act passed by which the Common Council are made *ex officio* members of the Public School Society, and thus constituted them parties and judges in the cause.

Let me not be misunderstood. I do not suppose for a moment that any gentleman of that Common Council would at any time knowingly deviate from the path of justice and duty on account of his official connexion with that Society; but at the same time I do know, that there is a powerful influence in association, against which the laws, with great wisdom, have guarded the judicial Bench, when they declare that a Judge should be of a single mind—elevated above all selfish considerations—and whose interests could never be affected by the result of any official act which he might be called on to execute, or any sentence which it might be his duty to pronounce. Here, then, were Aldermen of different parties elected from time to time, and so made members—part and parcel—of this Society ; and, I ask, would it have been a gracious thing in them, after having been so honored with a place in it, to become adverse to the interests of that body ? Let us bear in mind, too, that there is with most people a regard for consequences, and no Alderman could imagine he would greatly benefit his interests by opposing a corporation that has acquired nearly the entire control of all the public money appropriated for the purpose of education in New York, and having its dependents spread from one end of the city to the other. I think it would require a strong and elevated mind—an unusual amount of moral courage, to enable any man so situated to oppose such a Corporation.

I do not then admit the reasoning of Mr. Ketchum, for I deny his premises that the Common Council ever were " the representatives of the people" on this subject.

I will now commence my review of this speech. I read it carefully from beginning to end, and I was myself impressed with the idea that it scarcely required an answer. I was quite convinced of that, so far as the honorable Senators were concerned, because I knew that to the minds of men accustomed to reasoning, and to detect at a glance where the strength of a position rested, that speech must have appeared a thing altogether out of place. Nevertheless, it was hinted to me that the speech was not intended for Senators alone, and the readiness with which Mr. Ketchum could furnish the Report went considerably to strengthen that opinion. It was said, that though to me the speech might seem weak, yet to the generality of readers, particularly those unacquainted with the subject, it might seem very specious, and produce in their minds the very conclusions opposite to those which we would wish to see established. On that ground I have taken it up; and I must say that with regard to Mr. Ketchum himself, I have the kindest possible feeling, and if in the course of my remarks I should happen to speak in a manner seemingly disrespectful, I beg that it may not be considered as having been so intended: of the gentleman himself I cannot say any thing disrespectful—of his speech I hope I am permitted to say whatever the evidence may authorize. I mention his name with perfect freedom, because his name is attached to the speech, and because, principally, he is the official organ of that Society, and what he says is already endorsed by them.

After his introduction, Mr. Ketchum says:—

"This probably may account very sensibly for the fact, that in the city of New-York the portion of the school fund alloted to her was to be distributed by these almoners of her charity whom her representatives thought proper to designate. Now, I ask, was there any thing inconsistent with sound principle in this? Is there any thing in it which violates the principle of the largest liberty, and the purest democracy, of which we hear something in this report?"

Stop, Mr. Ketchum! I tell you that there is not one word in that whole Report against such a state of things as that you represent to the minds of the Senators, by making a wrong application. What is represented as contrary to the principle of our constitution, was the monopoly—the exclusive system that has succeeded to the former; and Mr. Ketchum is kind enough to make an anterior reference to the period when all enjoyed the appropriation for the purposes of education. I stop him there, and say, that he makes a wrong application. He ought not to prejudice the minds of Senators, or the community, by pretending that the Secretary's Report trenches on the enjoyment of the largest liberty.

Mr. Ketchum goes on.—

"In the city of New-York, as I shall have occasion to show by-and-bye—and more or less I suppose it is so in all the states of Christendom—there are voluntary associations—charitable associations—associations composed of men, incorporated or otherwise, who are willing to proffer their services; to feed the hungry; to clothe the naked; to visit the destitute, and to see to the application of funds set apart for their relief. Such men are always to be found in large cities; men of fortune, men of leisure, men of benevolence, who are willing to associate together for benevolent objects, and who are usually made the almoners of the charity of others."

Now, Mr. Ketchum, in the whole of this, is gliding imperceptibly to the point he wishes to reach. And what is that point? It is to fix on the minds of the Senators, that as religious societies formerly took care of their poor, and as other associations take care of other objects of benevolence, so they were to look upon the Public School Society as taking care of education. In endeavoring to effect this conclusion, his reasoning glides imperceptibly, as on a colored surface which is black at one extremity, and white at the other, but in which the various shades are so nicely mingled that you cannot ascertain the point where the change of color begins, so does the progress of his sophistry elude observation. "Charitable Associations." Now, I will examine Mr. Ketchum's philosophy here. I consider that there is here what may be called a rhetorical picture. He personifies the city of New York, and calls it "she"—then he takes her and places her on one side, and places all the religious societies, and benevolent societies —the Public School Society amongst the rest; and that being done, he says, the city of New York made them her "almoners." But when we take these societies away, where is "she?" what becomes of her?

(Laughter and cheers.)   This is what I call a rhetorical fiction.   **Mr. Ketchum** need not pretend to say that the city of New York made "almoners."   They were self-created.   When you take the religious societies, each having its charity school, and this Society, which we must not call irreligious, although it has always defeated its opponents by saying that they profess religion—these constitute the people of New York, and they received the money set apart for that specific purpose, and in their sovereign power and wisdom they applied it as they thought proper.   They managed it with perfect harmony, for I never heard of the occurrence of a dispute when each section of the community assumed the management of their own schools, and it was on account of a charge against one society of misappropriating the public money that the controversy arose.

Afterwards referring to the Legislature by which that state of things was changed to the present, he says :—

"Hence, after many discussions in the Assembly chamber, (discussions at which all the members were invited to attend—and almost all of them did attend —for we had generally a *quorum*, although it was before a committee night after night—the committee of the Assembly at length made a report favourable to the prayer of the memorial, but suggesting in that very report whether even so much as was granted in the proposition referred to was not a violation of sound principle; whether in fact religious societies ought to participate in the enjoyment of the fund at all, because, by such participation, the Jew might be made to support he doctrine of the Christian, and, *vice versa*, the Christian that of the Jew, the Catholic of the Protestant, the Protestant of the Catholic, and so on."

What a splendid discovery!   The people hitherto living in perfect harmony, all enjoying that appropriation of public money—not perhaps expending it in the wisest manner, but at all events without disturbance or dispute.   But all at once it is discovered that because they are religious societies, it would be a violation of sound principle to allow them the public money?   And why?   Because in that case the money paid by a Protestant might pass to the support of a Catholic school—or, if you please, to the school of a Jew—and that involved a violation of conscience.   I confess, however, I cannot see that, nor do I think any reflecting man can see it.   But what is the fact respecting the turn of the legislation in relation to the Public School Society, called, at that time, the "Free School Society?"   Simply, that because at that Bethel Baptist church, money had been improperly appropriated, occasion was taken to punish not the guilty party, if there was guilt, but those who had memorialized against the abuse of public money, and to disfranchise every man professing religion, because the members of one particular church had abused their trust!   And it is suspected that all this was not done without the secret instrumentality of that very Free School Society itself, which then, as at the present day, professed to have *no religion at all.*   So that in this very Legislature—though I know that another view of it is perfectly lawful—we see that the reasoning approved by Mr. Ketchum, would go to brand a stigma on the sacredness of religion—it would lead to the inference that because the adherents of one religious sect have abused their trust in the employment of the public money, that, therefore, all profession of religion should be an everlasting disqualification?   But I pronounce such an inference unworthy the citizens of a land in whose constitution Christianity is recognized. And I ask, where was the usual penetration of Mr. Ketchum when he employed such reasoning? By the laws of this State, church property is exempted from taxation ; and I am surprised that gentlemen of such tender apprehensions can rest quietly at night, when they reflect, that possibly Protestant money is going to make up the deficiency in the revenues of the State caused by the exemption from taxation granted to Catholic churches ! But I see no harm at all in the state of things by which money is thus transferred. All the churches are represented by all the people, and it matters not an iota if churches are exempted, the tax is paid by the members in another form.

So with the Public School money. Although in the manipulation of the money, it might happen that the identical dollar paid by a Pro testant might pass into the treasury of a Catholic school, the Catholic dollar would go back to replace it in the Protestant school, it would be in the end all the same, for the question is not at all about the IDENTITY of the money. If the taxes could be kept separate, and the money paid by the Protestant go into the Protestant box, and the money paid by the Catholic go into the Catholic box, sure enough they would get their own money, but it would be all the same if no such care had been taken. Here I would refer to the case of chaplains in our prisons, &c. not one of whom is a Catholic, but who have often received the con- tributions of Catholics—have they ever complained that that was a vio- lation of the constitution ? Certainly not; and that practical view of the matter should have taught the gentleman the futility of his reasoning— that if the money of the one sect went into the hands of another it was all the same—it was the money of the *people* received from them in one form, and returned to them in another, allowing them in its em- ployment the noble and grand privilege— of which I trust they will not allow themselves to be deprived, no matter how they exercise it—of obeying the dictates of their own free consciences. (Cheers.)

In the course of his speech, the gentleman makes a grand display of all the sects that were set aside by the Society. Then he asks the Senate, " will this honourable body grant to Catholics what was de- nied to all these?" But there is a difference here, and what is it ? *There is not on record an instance of a complaint on the part of any of these sects that their rights of conscience were invaded.* Episco- palians never made any such complaint—nor did Presbyterians—nor Methodists—nor did any of the other sects,—but it happened, that they had Charity schools attached to their churches, and they thought, giving such education as the state required, they were entitled to their share of the state bounty. But very different was the case of the Catholics. And now, suppose the circumstances of the case were re- versed, and Catholics had the majority on which the Society de- pends, and would employ the power conferred by it, in forcing on the whole community Catholic books, and Catholic versions of the Bible, and give the children lessons about the burning of Servetus, and the ignorance of a whole nation in supposing the machine for winnowing corn to be an impious invention, and denouncing those employing it as guilty of a crime against the God who supplies the zephyrs and the breeze,—suppose that case, and that the aggrieved minority com- plained and applied for redress, I trust that on the face of the earth there would not be found a Common Council of Catholics who would refuse to listen to so just a prayer!

34

Mr. Ketchum says farther, when speaking of the action of the Common Council on this application, that it had been referred to a Law Committee ; and he quotes the decision of that Committee. We, knowing the manner in which our former applications were disposed of, need not, of course, be surprised at the manner in which this Report was expressed. To our last application, made in the spring of 1840, —when I was absent from this country—to the Board of Assistant Aldermen, the usual negative was given ; but then it is to be observed, that that Board was surrounded by the advocates of the Society, and these things which we have stated, and which they have since acknowledged, were *denied* by them—and on that denial was grounded the refusal of our application. The advocates of the Society denied, that there were any passages in their books with which we could find fault ; averred that they contain nothing disrespectful to our religion. But since then, they have been obliged to retract that, and to acknowledge repeatedly that in making these assertions they were not sustained by truth ; that there were passages in those books reflecting upon our faith ; that these passages had been taught to the children for years, and would have been retained till this very day, had it not been for our detection and exposure. But it was not at all surprising, that under the influence of a Society, stretching its gigantic branches over every quarter of the city, and hearing such assertions from its advocates, the Board should deny our claim. But let us glance at the conclusion which Mr. Ketchum draws from such denial ; he says : —

"That conclusion was ratified by their constituents ; and I believe that every one of the religious societies, or nearly so, excepting the Roman Catholics, acquiesced in that decision. But that society, year after year, has come before the Common Council and renewed their request for a separate portion of the school fund. With the best feelings for the applicants, in a spirit of kindness, with every disposition to do whatever could be done for them, year after year, and without respect to politics, whether the one party was in the ascendant, or the other party was in the ascendant, the Common Council have, with almost entire unanimity, disallowed that request ; and I believe that never in either Board, since the division of that body into two Boards, has there been but one dissenting voice raised against the ratification of that decision. Now, if the committee please— who have complained? The Roman Catholics."

I repeat, that I deny the philosophy of this reasoning. I deny, that in any case, that portion at least of the community that has petitioned for a reform of this system, ever looked to the Common Council as their representatives on this question. And another argument against Mr. Ketchum's position is, that this Public Council were partizans in the case in which they were called to deliver judgment. And I think that it would be well for that Public School Society and the Common Council, if the latter by their election to office are to be engrafted into the former, that the duty of judging between them and the community were delegated to disinterested parties.

Mr. Ketchum goes on to say :

"No disrespect was intended them. The Common Council, and every person engaged in the discussion of the question on behalf of the Common School Society, took great care to say, 'We do not reject you because you are Roman Catholics,' and as evidence of this truth, we give you the fact that we have rejected similar applications from powerful Protestants—but we reject your request because we believe that a sound general principle will not allow us to grant it."

So there was always a precaution observed. Indeed, I myself remarked that before the Common Council. They uniformly—with one exception—said, that they did not oppose us because we were Catholics. But Dr. Spring, with great magnanimity and candour, neglected to take the hint, but declared that he was apprehensive of our faith gaining ground. He would oppose us and preserve the Society as it was, even though the rights of the Catholics should be damaged, and that for his part he preferred the religion of Voltaire to that of Fenelon! The sentiment was indeed a black one, and it was rendered blacker by the brightness of the candour with which it was uttered.

Here again Mr. Ketchum states what is incorrect He says :—

" We have rejected similar applications from powerful Protestants "

I deny that. I refer him to the records of the Common Council, and I will venture to affirm that he will not find there one " similar application." And why ? Simply because there was no ground for any such application. For although one denomination of Protestants may differ from another, and may carry their attachment to their respective dogmas to great length, yet there is one common ground on which they all, so far as I know, without exception, meet. What is it ? That the Bible alone, as understood by each individual, is their rule of faith *They* could therefore unite on their Public School question so far as the Bible was concerned. But then they required, that Catholic children, whose creed never admitted that principle, should be taught that doctrine. They had not the same reason that we had to go before the Common Council. We felt, that we might as well at once give up to them our children and allow them to educate them as they pleased, as send them to their schools. I deny then the statement, that " similar applications " were made.

Mr. Ketchum proceeds : —

" I say that the Corporation has been desirous, so far as that body possibly could, so far as they felt themselves at liberty, consistently with the maintenance of a sound general principle, to accommodate these parties They have granted a privilege out of this fund to the Roman Catholic denomination, which has not been granted to any other. The Sisters of Charity, so called, under direction of the Roman Catholic Church, and connected with it, (I believe I am right—if not I should be happy to be corrected,) established a most benevolent institution in the city of New-York, called the Orphan's Asylum—the Roman Catholic Orphan's Asylum. They took into this institution poor and destitute orphans They fed and clothed them most meritoriously—and they thus relieved the city of New-York of the maintenance of many who would otherwise, probably, have been a charge upon it. After long discussion, and with some hesitancy, yet overcome by the desire to oblige, and aware of the limitation arising from the very nature of that institution, the Corporation did permit the Catholic Orphan Asylum to receive money from this fund; and during the last year it received some 1462 dollars for the education of about, one hundred and sixty-five children—in common with the institution for the blind, and the deaf and the dumb, and those other benevolent and Christian institutions which are altogether of a Catholic character in the most comprehensive acceptation of that term—as they are under no sectarian influence or government."

And pray what sort of an institution is the Protestant Orphan Asylum ? Is religion not taught there ? And yet Mr. Ketchum singles out the Catholic Orphan Asylum, and speaks of the favour conferred upon it, in order to show the liberality of the Common Council. We are indeed grateful to that body for having placed ours on the same footing with other institutions of a kindred character. But the Common Council have granted money to the Protestant Half Orphan Asylum, and

denied an application of a similar grant to the Catholics. How can Mr. Ketchum assert that a "privilege" has been granted to us exclusively·
In reference to our last application, Mr. Ketchum proceeds : —

"The subject, I repeat, underwent a very full and free discussion; and, after that had terminated, the Board of Aldermen gravely considered and discussed the subject; and at length, after some delay, came to the conclusion that they would go and visit the schools. Some of the members of the Board of Public Schools, feeling sensibly alive on the subject, expressed to me an apprehension that this was a mere evasion, and they feared that the question had now become mingled with politics. But I said, Wait, gentlemen, let them go and see your schools,— it is a natural desire—they ought to go. It is a great and delicate question, and they ought to be acquainted with it in all its details.

"They went and visited the Public Schools, and the Roman Catholic Schools, and they incorporated the result of their deliberations in a report which I have before me, and from which I shall quote by-and-bye. It is drawn up with great ability, and the decision was, with but one dissenting voice, that the prayer of the petition should be rejected, and it was rejected."

On this I remark, in reference to what I have, I believe, already referred to, that there has been always a panacea for every evil — the appointment of a committee to visit the schools. Why this is one of the easiest things in the world! A little training — a little arrangement — a judicious wink to the teachers — will prepare every thing, so that it will be very hard if a pleasing exhibition could not be got up in any one of these schools for one hour, on any day out of the three hundred and sixty-five in the year.

But this has been the invariable remedy — no looking at the wounds which the system was from year to year, and from day to day, inflicting on less favoured portions of the community — no visit to the back streets and miserable lanes of this city, in which so large a portion of its future inhabitants are grovelling in exposure to vice and degradation. Nothing of that was thought of. But the schools enriched and adorned by the expenditure of more than a million of money were inspected, and the gratified and approving visitors returned to the Common Council, to make their report, that it was an excellent system, perfect in its details and admirable in its workings, and it was only the absurd bigotry and extreme ignorance of the Catholics, that prevented them from reaping its benefits!

Then he compares with all this, the state of our humble schools :
Well, I will not pretend to say that the Catholic schools were in the best order. But here I remark, that whilst at every stage and step of the progress of this question, I have been obliged to controvert false statements, I can challenge them to point to a single instance in which they could dispute the truth of any of our documents. And now I will give a passing notice to that visit to the Catholic schools. Hear this statement :—This Committee say

— "We also visited three of the schools established by the petitioners, and we found them as represented, lamentably deficient in accommodations, and supplies of books and teachers;⁣ the rooms were all excessively crowded, and poorly ventilated; the books much worn, as well as deficient in numbers, and the teachers not sufficiently numerous, yet, with all these disadvantages, though not able to compete successfully with the Public Schools, they exhibited a progress which was truly creditable, and with the same means at their disposal, they would doubtless soon be able, under suitable direction, greatly to improve their condition."

Such is their testimony.

And now shall I pass over this opportunity of making a comparison? When questioned before the Senate, the Society stated that *they* could not get the children to come, and here are our schools crowded to excess! I can show you in a room, not much larger than the square of the distance between two of the columns supporting the gallery of this building in which we are now assembled, upwards of two hundred children crowded together! Yet the Public School Society are obliged to pay $1000 a year of public money to visitors for the purpose of gathering children to their schools. For the fact came out in the course of the investigation, that they paid that sum yearly to Tract distributors for the purpose I have stated, whilst we, in our poverty, could not find room or books or teachers for the multitudes of children that thronged upon us, and whom this exclusive system consigns to degradation and ignorance, and vice, unless something be done for them by others! (Cheers.)

Such is the testimony of that very Committee. And yet the decision to which they came, is quoted by Mr. Ketchum as proof that a "great principle"—of which no definition known is given from the beginning to the end of his speech,—prevented them from granting our petition. Well I have called your attention already, and would do so again, to a point that shows, as clear as noon-day, that this denial was not benevolent towards us, nor in accordance with equal-handed justice They had opposed us as a sect—as being Catholics. The Secretary of State, however,—a man, whose integrity of character, legal knowledge, and profound and statesmanlike views, have elevated him to the highest rank in the community,—placed the question on entirely different grounds. Mr. Ketchum, in the last sentence of his speech before the Common Council, declared, that to the Public School Society the discharge of their duties was rather a burthen, which nothing but the extreme benevolence of their nature had prompted them to assume, and unless they were saved from this continued agitation, they would throw it off. Well, Mr Spencer excludes all these objectionable features, and places the question on a broad basis, entirely removed from all sectarianism; and then where are these benevolent gentlemen who are burthened with their charge—these "humble almoners" of the public bounty? At Albany, ready for a new fight! Not for their Schools, but to oppose the Secretary; for Mr. Spencer only wishes to make education like the air we breathe, the land we live in,—like other departments of human industry and enterprise—free! He would not hold the balances so as to afford the least advantage to any party, but would make all equal, and secure to them the enjoyment of the rights established by the Constitution of the country; and who opposed him? The Public School Society. Their interests were not invaded, but they could not admit the principle that we were to receive education consistently with the laws of the State? Why? You will find that in the course of Mr Ketchum's speech, he says the Public School Society could not stand one day if education were made free! If the monopoly which they have wielded for sixteen years should be touched by the little finger of free trade, they would perish! "They cannot live a day" And, gentlemen, if they cannot live one day on the principles of justice and freedom, then I say, that half a day's existence is quite enough for their exclusive system.

We have seen that Mr. Ketchum has introduced the Committee to the Schools, and now he comes to the point:

"Who, then complain of the operations of this system? Our fellow-citizens, the Roman Catholics.

"Failing to get from the hands of a body thus constituted, the redress for the grievance, which they complained of, they come here and now ask it of you. I say *they* come here, because I will presently show you from their memorials, that none *but* they come here."

He has brought it round to that, and he thinks that if that be established, the same prejudices, the same means, that were employed to defeat us in New-York, would be equally efficacious at Albany.

He says:

"Failing to accomplish their purpose through the Common Council of the City of New York, they come and ask it here. Failing in their application to a body of representatives to whom they have applied year after year, and who represent a population in which is intermingled a greater mass of Roman Catholic voters than in any other district of the State of New York"

See the advantage that he takes of our known forbearance, and their activity. Because we, with honourable motives that should have been better appreciated, abstained from making this question a political one. But they did make it such a question, and endeavoured to deter all public men from rendering justice to the oppressed Catholics.

Now I am no politician, I belong to no party, and I can also, perhaps, speak with the greater freedom, because we have high minded friends and opponents too, amongst both political parties, and I can perhaps give a satisfactory answer to Mr. Ketchum's allusion to " voters."

After the election of the Governor, the papers in the views of this Society, referred to it as a warning, and not only so, but individuals here, wrote to the Governor in terms of reproach against the Catholics and the Irish, for not having been more grateful to him. They taunted him with it. And how is that to be answered? I should be sorry that ever the Irish should be ungrateful under any circumstances, or ever forget a friend: and especially at a time when the high and noble principles of justice and equality laid down by the fathers of this country, seem to be passing rapidly into oblivion. If a public man stands up for the *rights* of even the humblest portion of the community, he is entitled to the gratitude and esteem of every man who loves his country. Not that the Governor conferred on us any peculiar favour. I disclaim that—he never asked any thing for us, but what we conceived our right. But still he was taunted with references to the ingratitude of the Irish. It was said, " there is what you got by advocating the cause of the Irish!" That shows whether we made our question a political one; and I am glad in one sense that the Irish did not vary from the principles in politics, to which they had been in the habit of attaching themselves. Because that demonstrates, that whatever may be the opinion of calculating politicians respecting the Irish, that portion of this community have, perhaps, after all, an integrity of character, and purity of principle, which is not unfrequently found wanting amongst more elevated classes of both political parties. It was discovered then, that the Irish would not abandon their principles from selfish motives. But now let me ask what was the case on the other side? Many of them turned quietly round, abandoning all their old political

. associations and friends, in order to let Gov. Seward know how much he had *dared* when he declared for justice and equal rights to all. (Cheers)

Such was the case, and our opponents cannot deny it. Mr. Ketchum then is unfortunate in his allusion. He ought not — if he had what I shall not now mention—if he had had presence of mind, I will say he ought not to have alluded to that matter at all, because it has brought up the proofs of what was done by his own clients, whilst our vindication is triumphantly effected.

We have thus been enabled to refute all the charges urged against us from the pulpits and religious presses, at the disposition of the Society, that we made a political question of it, and so forth. They did, but we did not.

Gentlemen, I have dwelt longer on some topics than I intended, and made less progress in my review of this speech than I anticipated. On to-morrow evening I will proceed with my remarks. (Loud, and long continued applause.)

The meeting then adjourned.

(On Friday evening, the Bishop attended, according to his intimation at Carroll Hall, and where, notwithstanding the extreme inclemency of the weather, a very considerable audience was assembled. It was, however, deemed expedient to adjourn the meeting till the following Monday)

MONDAY EVENING.

On Monday evening an immense number of persons assembled to hear the conclusion of the Right Rev. Prelate's speech. The aisles and galleries of the large building in which the audience congregated, were densely crowded, and in the body of the house it was impossible to obtain a seat for a considerable time before the meeting was organized. Amongst those present we noticed the Lieutenant Governor of this State, and many distinguished Senators.

Shortly before 8 o'clock, Thomas O'Connor, Esq. was called to the Chair amid the acclamations of the meeting ; and after the minutes of the former meetings had been read by B O'Connor, Esq. the Secretary, Bishop Hughes, rose and was received with deafening applause. On its subsidence, he proceeded as follows :—

Mr. Chairman and gentlemen, I have had occasion already to observe that the question we are now discussing has passed, or at least is now passing through the second stage of its progress. In the first stage we had to apply to the city authorities ; and we were obliged by the circumstances of the case, and for reasons that I have already mentioned, to apply in a character which we did not desire, but which was forced upon us by circumstances over which we had no control. The issue of that application is known. Then we laid our grievances before the Legislature of the State ; and the Secretary of State, to whom the question had been referred, placed it upon grounds altogether different from those on which it had hitherto been considered. Consequently it was necessary for me, in reviewing Mr. Ketchum's speech, to consider it under two heads. And hitherto my remarks on it have applied to the question under the circumstances in which it was, previous to its reference to the Legislature of the State. We have now, however to consider it on the ground on which it has been placed in the able and eloquent and liberal report of the Hon. Mr. Spencer. And I cannot avoid observing in the first place, that taking into account the principles of equality and of justice that pervade that document, I did conceive that the Public School Society could not have found any objections against it. For you will recollect that Mr. Spencer removes entirely the objections urged before the Common Council against the recognition of our claims. These objections were grounded on the principle that no sect or religious denomination had any thing to do with the money appropriated for the purpose of education. The Secretary has completely obviated that objection. He has regarded the petitioners in their civil capacity. He has exhibited the broad and general grounds on which every public institution in this country is conducted, but we find these gentlemen, nevertheless, as zealous, and their advocate as eloquent against Mr. Secretary Spencer as they had been against us There can be no charge now, that a recognition of our claims would favour sectarianism—a union of Church and State. All that has disappeared, and with it we had hoped would have disappeared the opposition to our claims.

I will now follow Mr. Ketchum in his arguments before the Senate. And first of all I would direct your attention to the number of times in which he repeats, that the petitioners are Catholics. He twists and turns that in a variety of ways, in order to convince the Senators, that though we applied in the character of citizens, that advantage was to be taken away from us, and we were to be clothed before that honourble body with our religious character, by the hand of Mr. Ketchum! I should have less confidence in the stability of this government — less affection for its constituted authorities, if I thought that such a circumstance could militate against us in the minds of those gentlemen, who have been elected by the suffrages of the people to the guardianship of equal rights. (Cheers) I conceive, therefore, that Mr. Ketchum has mistaken the character of that assembly — that he has exerted himself in vain to fix on us the epithet of Roman Catholics, when we appeared in the character of citizens, and when our right to worship God according to the dictates of our conscience had been already, a priori, recognized by the constitution of the country. And I ask is there any crime in being a Roman Catholic? Is there any advantage to be gained in bringing that against us? Is there any thing in the history of the country which could justify the hope of prejudicing the minds of Senators by such an allusion? No In the days when men stood side by side, and shoulder to shoulder, and blood touched blood in the battle strife, and with their brave swords they won the freedom of their country was it asked who is a Catholic, or who is a Protestant? (Loud cheers.) Had Mr. Ketchum forgotten the names and deeds of Kosciusko, of Pulaski, of Lafayette, and the Catholic soldiers of Catholic France? Was there any thing said against that religion by the fathers of our country, when they laid the foundation of the liberties we now enjoy? Was there any such charge against Charles Carroll, when he came and signed that glorious Declaration, risking more than all the other signers together? No. Nor have we any cause to be ashamed of our religion, and God forbid we ever should! I throw back, then, that manoeuvre of Mr. Ketchum, and I tell him, this is not the country whose constitution makes apparent to the world, that to be a Roman Catholic involves a deprivation of the rights and privileges of citizenship

Last year a petition was presented to the Senate, signed by Catholics alone—this year the petition had other signatures. True, the petitioners were generally Catholics, but others signed it too; and I hope and believe, that they thought they asked but for justice. However, Mr. Ketchum, in order to accomplish his purpose, takes up the petition presented last year, and taunts the Secretary, as if he were guilty of artifice in making it appear, that the members of other religious denominations had joined in our petition. He says.

" Probably, (continued Mr. Ketchum,) that circumstance was discovered by the Secretary's sagacity, between 1840 and 1841 "

What does he mean by that allusion except to remind the Secretary, that it was by prejudicing the public mind by misrepresentations, that certain partizans succeeded in diminishing the vote for his Excellency the Governor? If Mr. Ketchum does not intend that by this delicate hint, I should like to know what he does mean. He then affects to take up the objections .—

" One of the complaints is that the people are not represented in this Public School Society , that here is an agency used for a great public purpose which the people do not directly choose , and they complain of the Public School Society being a close corporation "

Certainly, all these are grounds of complaint, and all these are so clearly set forth in the Report of the Secretary, that you have but to read that document to see that Mr. Ketchum cannot shake one solitary position of that honourable gentleman. Is not the Public School Society a close corporation? And is not Mr. Secretary Spencer's Report calculated to place it on the same basis on which all our free public institutions are founded? Is the Secretary not a Reformer, then, in reference to that Society? He does here precisely what Lord John Russell attempts to do in England, when he endeavours to break down the monopoly of the corn laws, and to make bread cheap—Mr. Spencer wishes to break down the monopoly of education, and to make voting and education, the bread of knowledge, cheap. That is to say, that the same people who are supposed to be capable of choosing a Sheriff, or a Governor, or a President, without paying for the privilege, should also have the right of choosing the teachers of their children without paying $10 for it. (Cheers) Mr. Ketchum passes over that very lightly. That is a point not to be seriously dwelt upon, and he glides into the old charge preferred before the Common Council, and takes up the old objections, although not one of them was presented in the petition before the Senate. Keeping always before the mind of the Senators, that we are Catholics, he affects to take up these objections, and says .—

" Now, I wish to call the attention of the Committee to the fact now to he stated,—there is no complaint in these memorials, nor will you hear any from any source, that the Public School Society does not furnish to all the children who attend their schools a good literary education."

Let me caution Mr. Ketchum not to be so fast, and I will give him my reasons From the manner in which the examinations are conducted, it is the easiest thing in the world to have all ready prepared for the day of visitation ; when the examiners present themselves, *pet classes* are arranged, and in them *pet pupils*, who will perform their part admirably well. It is easy to have all this array, and so it is to be regarded rather as an exhibition, than an examination. But if they desire their examinations to create universal confidence, let them have them as they are conducted in European universities, where the pupils stand forward, and any person who chooses, examines them; when not the choice and prepared pupils are taken, but the subjects of examination are selected indiscriminately from the classes. Let such a method be adopted here, and I will venture to say that Mr. Ketchum will not have any thing to boast of over other schools. (Cheers.) I do not, however, blame the visitors for not finding fault with the external management of these schools. I think it excellent—and the best proof of the sincerity of that opinion, was afforded in our willingness to adopt, and place the superintendence of our schools in the hands of these very gentlemen.

But Mr. Ketchum goes on :—

"The Roman Catholics complain, in the first place, that they cannot conscientiously send their children to the Public Schools, because we do not give religious instruction in a definite form, and of a decided and definite character. They complain, in the second place, that the school books in common use in the Society, contain passages reflecting upon the Roman Catholic Church And they complain, in the third place, that we use the Bible without note or comment —that the school is opened in the morning by calling the children to order and reading a chapter in the Bible,—our common version. These are the three grounds on which they base their conscientious scruples"

Now it is a fact that we do not complain of any one of these things in our petition to the Senate. One of these complaints was expressed in the petition to the Common Council, and I have alalready explained the reasons of that presentation. But in the petition to the Senate, we said in general terms, that the conscientious scruples of a large portion of our fellow-citizens were violated by the system pursued in these schools. I will however take up these objections in order.

Mr. Ketchum says that we complain in the first place, that we cannot send our children to the schools of the Public School Society, "because religion is not there taught of a decided and definite character." Mr. Ketchum certainly has not stated the objection correctly, for I defy him to find such words in our petition. We complained in general against these schools, that by divorcing religion and literature, they endangered the best interests of children who were to grow up to be men, and who to be useful members of the community, should have their minds imbued with correct principles, and could not be so without being made acquainted with some religious principles. But we never complained that they did not give "definite religious instruction." Far from it, and when Mr. Ketchum asserted that we did, I am sorry say that he asserted what he must or might have known to be untrue. And how do I prove it? In our propositions to the Committee of the Common Council, when they had gone through with their ceremony of visiting the schools, and the Society had offered their propositions, the very last article of our proposal was in these words. "*But nothing* of their (i. e. Catholic) *dogmas, nothing against the creed of any other religious denomination shall be introduced.*" Mr. Ketchum saw that, and I ask him, how

could he undertake to make an argument by substituting language entirely different from ours, and presenting it as our objection? How could he say that we found fault with the Public School
Society for not teaching religion in a " definite form," when they
always disclaimed the right to teach it at all, and considered it a
crime for any denomination to ask for it? This is what I call
substitution—invention—a course unworthy of Mr. Ketchum, of
his profession, and of that Society of which he was the organ.

I am well aware that to a hasty reader, Mr. Ketchum's speech
will appear very logical indeed. But I have at the same time, to
observe that while he reasons logically, by drawing correct infer-
ences from his premises, he has taken care previously, to change
the premises, and instead of taking our principle as submitted by
us, he gradually shifts it—preserving however, enough to de-
ceive a cursory reader, until he substitutes one entirely different,
from which he reasons very logically of course. Let us suppose
Mr. Ketchum a professor of Law in some Uuniversity—for I
have no doubt he could fill such a chair, and adorn it too, if he
would; and imagine him addressing a class of students. He
says "Gentlemen, one of the most important things in our profession is to know how to conduct an argument, which you must
always do with logical precision. And to effect this, you are to
follow this excellent rule—if your facts sustain your conclusions
well—if not, you must find other facts that will!" (laughter and
loud cheers.) " The principle of this rule, I call, the principle
of, substitution—and an admirable principle it is—but you must
be cautious how you use it, especially before a Judge and Jury.
But if it is before a public, which reads fast—for there is a great
deal to be read—you will find it work very well. Recollect then,
gentlemen, this great principle—" substitute " in your reasoning!" (loud laughter.)

In such a way, we might imagine Mr. Ketchum addressing his
students. And you will find that few reason illogically. Even
the inmates of the Lunatic Asylum reason very logically. One
of them perhaps, imagines himself a clock, he says " Stand off,
don't shake me, I am obliged to keep time." That is logical reasoning. The only mistake is, that he " substitutes " a clock for
a living creature—and reasoning from this substitution, he draws
the conclusion admirably. So it is with Mr. Ketchum. (Laugh
ter and cheers.)

We did not, I tell Mr. Ketchum ask the Public School Society to
teach religion in any definite form. We never complained of
their not teaching it. We never did ask such an unreasonable
thing from men who made it a crime for *religious* societies to
have anything to do with the public money.

He then states another objection—" that the books used in the
schools, contain passages reflecting on the Catholic Church."
That is true; and he says in the third place, that we object that
" the Protestant version of the Bible is used, and that the schools
are opened by calling the children to order, and reading a passage from that Bible." Not a word of that in our petition.
That is " substitution " again—removing the objections present-

cd by us, and substituting others which might, as he supposed, lead to the denial of our claims, on the ground that we object unreasonably.

Mr. Ketchum takes up the objection, and in order to show how unreasonable that was, he submits the proposition of the Public School Society—passsing altogether over ours, which common justice required, should have been also presented, as it would have discovered on our part a similar disposition, and have entirely undeceived the Senators, as to any alleged claim to have religion taught in a definite form.

There was no official declaration guarding against the possibility, that, next year, another board might alter all these books to a worse state than ever ; and consequently their offer to expunge their books was altogether nugatory. Mr. Ketchum says however—

" This portion of the report, as will be seen, has reference to these offensive passages. Now, every body will say, that it is a fair off'r—we will strike them out But, gentlemen of the committee, I submit whether here, in this country, we must not in matters of conflicting opinions, give and take a little "

Well, I do not find the Public School Society, although very good at *taking*, at all disposed to *give* any thing (Laughter.)

" I have no doubt that I can find something in any public school book, of much length, and containing much variety of matter, reflecting upon the Methodists—upon the heated zeal, probably of John Wesley, and his followers—reflecting upon the Episcopalians, the Baptists, and Presbyterians. Occasional sentences will find their way into public discourses, which, if viewed critically, and regarded in a captious spirit, rather reflect upon the doctrines of all those churches "

In this way he gets over these passages, most insulting to us and our religion, which I pointed out to these gentlemen, after their having inculcated them in the minds of the children for sixteen years past ! We have to add however, that in examining these books, we found no passages reflecting on those denominations.

Now I will call your attention to Mr Ketchum's views respecting conscience and conscientious scruples. *We* supposed, that when a man could not do a thing in conscience, the reason was, that he thought by doing it, he would offend God This is what we supposed to be a conscientious difficulty ; and therefore it was that we did not object (as he says, and as I shall have occasion to treat of presently) to the Protestants reading *their* version of the Bible ; because, believing it right, they could use it with a good conscience But we Catholics did not approve of that version—many other denominations do not approve of it—the Baptists and Unitarians, for instance—and our objection, was that Mr Ketchum and the Public School Society would *force on us* the reading of that version against which we had conscientious objections. We believe that to yield to that, would damage the faith which we hold to be most pleasing to God. Suppose us to be in error, if you please, but certainly the Public School Society have no right to rule that we are. They are not infallible, and consequently should recognize our right of conscience, as we recognize theirs

But Mr. Ketchum has battled bravely against these principles, and thinking it would be better for us to agree to offend our God, and coincide with the Public School Society, wishes to beat down these scruples And now would you have *his* idea of a conscientious scruple ? He institutes a comparison, in order to show how trifling such things are, and he says :—

" On the other hand, there are many passages from the speeches of Mr Webster, which have found their way into school books , and a democrat may say, I cannot go Mr Webster , my children shall not be taught to admire him   And thus, if we are captious, we can find conscientious scruples enough."

So that Mr Webster's writings are placed, as it were, on a parallel with the word of God himself ; and a difficulty of which he is the subject, is spoken of in the same way as if it were a difficulty in reference to God ' And what is Mr. Ketchum's conclusion ? That, whilst he would trample on our conscientious scruples about the Deity, he bows with great deference to the scruple about Mr. Webster, and of this he goes on :—

" However, if it is bona fide a conscientious scruple, there is the end of it , we cannot reason with it   But, in the judgment of the Common Council, and as I think must be the case in the judgment of every man, the difficulty is got over by the proposition which has been made "

Well now just let him extend a little of that indulgence to us, in the case in which our account to our Creator and eternal Judge is involved. But not so   He next says :—

" The next complaint is, that we do not give religious education enough."

Where did Mr Ketchum find that ? That is "substitution," again He has not found that in any thing from us   He proceeds :—

" The memorials, all of which are public—and the speeches and documents which have been employed, and which, if necessary, can be furnished to the committee—all go conclusively to demonstrate that, in the judgment of those who spoke for the Roman Catholic Church, we ought to teach religion in our public schools—not generally—not vaguely—not the general truths of religion ; but that specific religious instruction must be given   Now, I hardly suppose that this deficiency can be made the subject of conscientous objection "

But that is a false issue. On none of these points has he stated our objection. We never objected, as far as Catholic children were concerned, that *they* did not teach religion. We complained of a system from which religion was (according to them) excluded BY LAW. But that, on the contrary, they did attempt sureptitiously to introduce such teaching, in a form that we did not recognize. What does he say then ?—

" The third and last complaint is, that our Catholic brethren cannot consent to have this Bible read in the hearing of their children   Now, on every one of these points, the trustees have been disposed to go as far as they possibly could in the way of accommodation; but they never yet consented to give up the use of the Bible to the extent to which it is used in the schools. I say the trustees have never yet consented to this surrender. But if they can have good authority for doing it, they will do it
" If the Legislature, by its own act, will direct that the Bible shall be excluded, I will guaranee that it shall be excluded '

Now, perhaps one of the rarest talents of an orator is that which enables him to accommodate his discourse to the character of the audience whom he addresses   But, like all rare talents, it should be exercised with discretion   That the learned gentleman possesses it, however, is proved by the fact, that the very declarations made by him before the Senate, are contradicted by his statements before the Common Council, and *vice versa*. Before the Common Council, in the presence of a number of the clergy, he eloquently denounced the exclusion of the Bible from the schools. If a compromise depended on this, he must say, " NO COMPROMISE !" Before the. Senate, however, he is all obsequiousness. "Gentlemen, if you give us authority to exclude the Bible, I guarantee that it shall be so " [Cheers]

I recollect the beautiful period with which the gentleman wound up his sentiments before the Common Council. I remember him saying that " it would be hard to part with that translated Bible—hard indeed, for it had been the consolation of many in death, the spring of hope in life, and wherever it had gone there was liberty and there was freedom; and where it had not gone, there was darkness and there was despotism." But I must apologize for attempting to repeat, as I spoil the poetry of his eloquent language. At the time, however, I thought what a beautiful piece of declamation that would be at a Bible Society meeting ; for on such occasions, owing to the enthusiasm—the sincere enthusiasm of the auditors—and the oftentimes artificial enthusiasm of the speakers, all history, philosophy, and common sense occasionally, are rendered quite superfluous. The most beautiful phrases, resting on no basis but fancy, may be strung together, and will produce the deepest impression. But I doubt much, when we come to examine the sober reality of the matter, whether the poetical beauties of Mr. Ketchum's picture will not be seen vanishing into thin air. I doubt much, indeed, whether the liberty whose origin and progress history has recorded, will be found to have sprung from "that translated Bible," in any sense, and especially in the sense of Mr. Ketchum. I, of course, yield to no man in profound veneration for the book of God ; but there is a point of exaggeration which does no credit, but injury, to that holy book.

Let us look at these translations of the Bible. The first was Tyndall's, then Coverdale's, and then the Bishop's Bible; these remained till the time of James the First ; and during all that time, a period of about a century—if ever there was a period of degrading and slavish submission to tyranical power in England, it was then beyond all comparison. At the close of this period, a new translation was made, and dedicated to the king. It was discovered that the "only rule of faith and practice" during all this time was full of errors and corruption. Every one knows that James was one of the poorest of the poor race from whom he was descended. Yet in their dedication, the translators appointed to amend the Rule of Faith by a new translation, call him the "Sun in his strength," and " that from his many and extraordinary graces, he might be called " THE WONDER OF THE WORLD."

Now, during the succeeding sixty or eighty years what were the doctrines of liberty in England? It was then that the schoolmen of Oxford and Cambridge taught from that translated Bible the dogma of " NONRESISTANCE to the ROYAL AUTHORITY"—that " PASSIVE OBEDIENCE" was the duty of subjects—that no crime nor possible tyranny of the prince, could authorize a subject to rebel. How could Mr. Ketchum forget all that?

Let us examine the facts of the case, and ascertain how correct Mr. Ketchum is when he said that liberty had always followed the progress of that translated Bible. You will find that from the period of the Reformation, down to the period of the Revolution, England was sunk to the lowest degree of slavish submission to tyranical authority. The spirit of old English freedom had disappeared at the Reformation, and it was only at the Revolution, that, like a ship recovering its equilibrium after having long been capsized, by the storm that old spirit righted itself again. But do I speak poetry like Mr. Ketchum? let me appeal to facts. (loud cheers.)

We find the fudamental principles of liberty as well understood by our Catholic ancestors, centuries before the reformation, as they are at the present day. They well understood the principles that all civil authority is derived from the people, and that those elected to exercise it, are reponsible to those from whom they derive their power.

" By one of the laws of Edward the Confessor, confirmed by the Conqueror, the duties of the king are defined, and it is provided, that, UNLESS he should properly discharge them, he should not be allowed even the name of king as a title of courtesy, and this on the authority of a pope The coronation of Henry I was based on as regular a contract as ever yet took place in market-overt. By the coronation oaths of the several monarchs between him and John, a similar contract was implied. By Magna Charta, and its articles for keeping the peace between the king and the kingdom, this implied contract was reduced to writing, and, ' signed, sealed, and delivered by the parties thereto ' In the reign of Henry III, Bracton, one of his judges, tells us, that since the king ' is God's minister and deputy, he can do nothing else on earth, but that only which he can do of right   Therefore, while he does justice, he is the deputy of the Eternal King, but the minister of the devil, when he turns to injustice   For he is called king from governing well, and not from reigning , because he is king while he reigns well, but a tyrant, when he violently oppresses the people entrusted to him   .   . Lc. the king, therefore, allow to the law what the law allows to him,—dominion and power,—for he is not a king, with whom his will, and not the law, rules,"—DUBLIN REVIEW.

There was the language of a Judge in the times before either the Reformation or James' translation of the Bible were dreamed of! I pass to another historical event—the crowning of John, on which occasion Hubert, the Archbishop of Canterbury, fearing that the monarch, from supposing that his royal blood alone entitled him to receive the kingly office, should throw the kingdom into confusion, reminded him that no one had such *a right* to succeed another in the government unless chosen by the people.

" That no one had a right by any precedent reason to succeed another in the sovereignty, unless he were unanimously chosen by the entire nation, and pre-elected according to the eminency of his morals, after the example of Saul, the first anointed king, whom God had set over his people, though not a king's son or sprung of a royal race, that thus he who excel'ed all in ability, should preside over all with power and authority. But if any of a deceased king's family excelled the rest of the nation, to his election they should more readily assent For these reasons they had chosen Count John, the brother of their deceased king, on account as well of his merits as of his royal blood To this declaration, John and the Assembly assented "

I wonder whether an Archbishop of Canterbury, now, with this translated Bible in his hands, would *dare* to utter such language in the presence of the monarch, when he was about to officiate at a coronation! Let us now turn to what occurred after this translation of the Bible. At the execution of the Earl of Monmouth, there were a number of Protestant divines who exhorted him to die like a " good christian," and the great point on which they insisted, was, that the subject was bound to obey the Prince, with " passive obedience.

But the noble Earl, in whose breast there still burned something of the principles of the olden times of England, could not agree to that dogma, and then the divines under the influence of this translated Bible, refused to pray for him. Their last words were

" Then, my lord, we can only recommend you to the mercy of God, but we cannot pray with that cheerfulness and encouragement as we should, if you had made a particular acknowledgment "

The same doctrine was prevalent in the time of Tillotson, and he speaks of it not only as his own opinion, but as that of those for whom Mr. Ketchum claims the honor of being considered the apostles of English liberty! I quote from the Dublin Review.

"Among those who importuned the unfortunate Lord Russell to make a similar acknowledgment, was Tillotson, who, by letter, told him that this doctrine of non-resistance, 'was the declared doctrine of all Protestant Churches, though some particular persons had thought otherwise,' and expressed his concern that you do not leave the world in a delusion and false hope to the hinderance of your eternal happiness,' by doubting this saving article of faith. Within the same period, Bishop Sanderson delivered the doctrine in the following clear and explicit language. He declares that, 'to blaspheme the holy name of God, to sacrifice to idols,' &c &c 'to take up arms against a lawful sovereign, none of these, and sundry other things of the like nature, being all of them simple and de toto genere, unlawful, may be done on any color or pretence whatsoever, the express command of God only excepted, as in the case of Abraham sacrificing his son, not for the avoiding of scandal not at the instance of any friend, or command of any power on earth—not for the maintenance of the lives and liberties of ourselves or others, nor for the defence of religion, nor for the preservation of the Church and State, no nor yet, if that could be imagined possible, for the salvation of a soul, no not for the redemption of the whole world.' This was considered a very orthodox effusion"

An article of faith that you dare not under any circumstances resist the kingly power!

Compare then the language of Protestant divines having this translated Bible before them, with that of Catholic divines at a former period, and see the ground which Mr Ketchum has found in England for his poetical assortion But perhaps if we turn our attention to the Protestant governments on the continent of Europe, we may find his dream realized. Perhaps he may find it realized in Prussia? In that country their are two principal communions of Protestants, the Lutheran and the Calvanist. Now the King calls his officers together, and tells them to draw up a liturgy—decrees that both *will* and *shall*, and *must* believe or practice this liturgy! [laughter and cheers.] Or he may go to Norway, or Sweden, or Denmark, and the dark despotism of the North, perchance there he may find that liberty, of which he speaks, progressing with this translation. What kind of freedom let me ask Mr. Ketchum, followed this "translated Bible" to Ireland—that everlasting monument of Catholic fidelity and Protestant shame! [tremendous applause.]

But to come to this country—perhaps it was in New England among the puritans, that Mr. Ketchum's dream was realized? ask the Quaker! [laughter] Perhaps it was Virginia—ask the Presbyterian! Where was it? Let me tell you. It was in Maryland among the Catholics. *They* knew enough of the rights of conscience to raise the first standard of religious liberty that ever floated on the breeze in America.

You may be told that Roger Williams, and his associates in Rhode Island, declared equal rights. Not at all—he excluded Roman Catholics from the exercising the elective franchise. But the Catholics did not exclude him. They may refer to Pennsylvania—the reference is equally unfortunate, for Penn wrote from England, remonstrating with the Governor Logan, I believe, for permitting the scandal of Catholic worship in Philadelphia. Turn now, look at the constellation of Catholic Republics, before Protestantism was dreamed of as a future contingency. Look at Venice, Genoa, Florence, and that little republic, not larger than a pins head on the map—San Marino—which has preserved its independence for such a long course of centuries, lest the science of republicanism should be lost to the world!

Look at Poland,—when the Protestants were persecuting one another to the death in Germany, Poland opened her gates to the refugees, and made them equal with her own subjects, and in the Diet of Poland, at which the law was passed, there were eight Catholic Bishops, and they must have sanctioned the law, for the liberism veto, gave each the power to prevent it. I challenge Mr. Ketchum to point, in the whole history of the globe, to one instance of similar liberality on the part of Protestants towards Catholics!

Now what becomes of that beautiful declaration of Mr. Ketchum, that wherever that translation had gone, liberty had followed? I know indeed, that in this country, we all enjoy equal, civil rights, but I know also that it was not Protestant liberality that secured them. They grew out of necessity; and in the declaration of them there is no difference made between one religion and another. Catholics contended as valiantly as any other in the first ranks of the contest for liberty. And I fervently hope, that it is too late in the day for any one to pretend that Catholics have been so blinded by their religion as to be unable to know what is liberty and what is not. (Cheers.)

Be it understood then, that not one of the objections which Mr. Ketchum has put into our mouths respecting the Bible, was presented to the Senate by us.

Mr. Ketchum after having thus disposed of our pretended objections, goes on to speak of the Secretary's Report:—

"They will be satisfied with it, it will give them what they ask. Now, let us see *how*. There is no proposition contained in this Report that religious societies, as such, shall participate in this fund—none."

Then, Sir, I ask what is your objection? In New York before the Common Council all your opposition was directed against "religious societies. Mr. Spencer has removed every ground for that, and I therefore ask what is your objection? Your object is to preserve the Public School Society in the possession of the monopoly, not only of the funds contributed by the citizens for the support of education, but also of the children. He says:—

"The trustees of districts shall indicate what religion shall be taught in those schools; that is to say, that you shall have small masses, that these small masses shall elect their trustees; and as the majority of the people in those small masses may direct, so shall be the character of the religious instruction imparted."

Mr. Spencer wishes to take from the Society that very feature which is objected to—that is to say, he wishes that religion shall neither be excluded nor enforced *by law*. And yet, Mr Ketchum, by his old principle of substitution, makes out quite a different proposition from the Report, and infers that the Trustees shall have the power to prescribe what religion shall be taught. I do not see that in the report at all. On the contrary, the Secretary leaves parents at liberty to act on that subject as they see proper. Mr. Ketchum supposes a case to illustrate his view of the matter, which I must say does not do him much credit. He says:

"But when a school is formed in the sixth ward of the city of New York, in which ward (for the sake of the argument we will assume) the Roman Catholics have a majority in the district; they choose their trustees and these trustees indicate that a specific form of religion, to wit, the Roman Catholic, shall be taught in that school—that mass shall be said there, and that the children shall cross themselves with holy water in the school, having the right to do so according to this Report, the Catholics being in a majority there. Then, and not till then, can these Roman Catholics conscientiously send their children to school—that is to say their objections to this system are to be overcome by having a school to which they conscientiously send their children, and that school must be one in which religion is to be taught according to their particular views."

That is drawing an inference without the facts, for we never said so; never even furnished him with authority to say so; and although Mr. Ketchum has the authority of the Public School Society *to speak*, yet that does not enable him, when he states what is not the fact, to make it true. But I wish to know why he brought up that picture at all; why the Sixth Ward should have peculiar charms in his imagination; or why he should have introduced all that about the children crossing themselves with holy water? And pray is it for Mr. Ketchum to find fault with what he supposes to be a religious error, and for which he is not at all accountable? He has not shown, nor has any man shown, that any such consequences would follow; it is impossible that the Trustees could act so ridiculously as to permit such a thing; it was incredible that they being responsible to the officers appointed by the State, and under the eye of such vigilant gentlemen as Mr. Ketchum, and the Public School Society, could permit mass to be celebrated in the school! Yet such is the picture presented by Mr. Ketchum, quite in accordance with his old course, and in order to excite popular prejudices, for which purpose this speech seems to have been so studiously prepared. For he well knew, that amongst a large portion of the Protestants, there is a vast amount of traditional prejudice against Catholics which has, from being repeated incessantly, and seldom contradicted, become fixed, occupying the place of truth and knowledge. Their case reminds me of what is related of Baron Manchausen. It is said, that when this celebrated traveller was old, he had a kind of *consciousness* that there was some former period of his life when he knew that all his stories were untrue, but he had repeated them so often that, now, he actually believed them to be true! (Loud laughter and cheers.)

It is to such persons as are under the influence of these prejudices and bigotries that Mr. Ketchum addresses his speech; and if he utter the sentiments of the Public School Society, how, I ask, can we confide to their hands the training of the tender minds of our children?

But one of the most remarkable things in this speech is, that after having beaten off in succession the different religious denominations, because, as he said, they would teach religion, having in fact played the one sect against the other. Mr. K. turns round and affirms that the Society itself does teach religion. He says:

"No, sir. I affirm that the religion taught in the public schools is precisely that quantity of religion which we have a right to teach, it would be inconsistent with public sentiment to teach less, it would be illegal to teach more."

The "exact quantity!" Apothecary's weight! (great laughter) Nothing about the quality, except that Mr. Ketchum having made it an objection that we wished religion in a definite form, he will give it an *indefinite* form —a fine religion—but at all events there is to be the "legal quantity." Well now let us see something about the quality of this religion—and I wish to consider the subject seriously. And here let me refer to a beautiful sentiment expressed by the Secretary in his Report. He says, that religion and literature have become so blended that the separation of the one from the other is impossible. A more true or appropriate declaration could not proceed from the lips of any man wishing the welfare of his country and his kind! (cheers)

Now whenever we made objections to that Society for pretending that religious subjects were excluded by law it was on these grounds. We said, we refer you to the experience of public men—to that of the most celebrated Statesmen in Europe, even the infidels of France, who have uniformly declared that society cannot exist except on the basis of religion. All of them whether believing in religion or not, have admitted the necessity of having some kind of religion as the basis of the social edifice. But these gentlemen, in all their debates, have contended, that the education to be given should be "purely civil and secular." That is their official language. And now for the first time, Mr. Ketchum before the Senate, declares that the Society does teach religion, and exactly the proper quantity!

Let me now call your attention to a passage in one of their reading books, in order that we may see a specimen of this religion. I will now make a few comments on the passage, but I do conceive that there are persons of all those denominations who recognize the doctrine of the Divinity, who could not be induced to have the minds of their children inoculated with such sentiments as it contains. Referring to our Blessed Redeemer, one of their school books says:

"His answers to the many insidious questions that were put to him, showed uncommon quickness of conception, soundness of judgment and presence of mind ; completely baffled all the artifices and malice of his enemies , and enabled him to elude all the snares that were laid for him "

Are these the ideas of the divine attributes of the Redeemer which the Christian portion of the community wish impressed on the minds of their children? That such have been the sentiments taught by the Society for the last sixteen eyars, they cannot deny. And they may account for it as they please, but it has attracted the attention of many, that for the last sixteen years, the progress of that young and daring blasphemy that trifles with all that is sacred, has increased ten fold in this city. How do I account for it? In two ways—first, because a large portion of the young are debarred from the benefits of education, and on the other hand, there is the attempt which has been made to divorce religion from literature When such causes exist, you need not be surprised to find that infidelity thickens its ranks and raises on every side its bold and impious front.

I have presented you with a specimen of the *quality* of that religion which Mr. Ketchum says is dealt out with exact and legal measure.

Mr. Ketchum contends that it is religion of a decided character that we want. And pray what are we to understand by a religion that is *not* decided? A religion which is vague—a general religion ? What is the meaning of these terms ? I desire to have a definition of them.

If there is to be established by law a Public-School-Society-religion, I should like to have its confession of faith, and be informed of the number of its articles, and the nature of the doctrines contained in them. But it seems to me, that Mr. Ketchum and this Public School Society resemble a body of men who are opposed to all physicians because they understand medicine; and who, although themselves opposed to all practice of medicine, are yet disposed to administer to the patients of the regular practitioners. And the comparison holds good—for, after all, children are born with a natural moral disease—want of knowledge, and evil propensities, and education and religion are the remedial agents to counteract these evil tendencies, and remove the natural infirmity. Then we have the practitioners, as they may be termed, coming to see the patient, the whole community supplying the medicine chest; and we have these men surrounding this chest and exclaiming to the physicians, " Clear off! you are a Thompsonian, and you are a Broussaist, and you are a Homopathic, and you are a regular practitioner, and you wish to prescribe remedies of a decided and definite character, which is contrary to 'a great principle,'"—and having thus banished all the physicians, they turn doctors themselves and mix up their drugs into what they call a " general medicine," of which they administer what they call the legal quantity. (laughter and cheers.) But the gentlemen forget that neither the patient nor the medicine are theirs. Those who furnish the patient and supply the medicine chest, should have a voice in the selection of the Doctors.

What do the gentlemen really intend ? They object to religious societies, but after they have got them pushed out of the house, they begin to teach religion themselves! Mr. Ketchum acknowledges that. He and Mr. Sedgwick, his associate, however, do not appear to have studied theology in the same school. One says, that religion is the basis of all morality, the other, that morality is the basis of religion. And after all, do men agree any more in their views of morality than religion ? Certainly not. And yet you must give to the children, especially those of that class attending these schools, for it should be borne in mind that they, for the most part, do not enjoy the opportunity of parental or pastoral instruction—some supply of religious education. They are the offspring of parents who, unfortunately, cannot supply that deficiency ; and if they are brought up in this way with a kind of contempt for religion, or with the most vague idea of it, the most lamentable results must necessarily follow.

I now come to another point—the non-attendance of the children in the schools. Whilst our humble school rooms are crowded to excess, the society has been obliged to give $1000 a year to persons for recruiting for children. In Grand street they have erected a spledid building, almost sufficient to accommodate the Senate of the State, and besides all that, we find that they are able to lavish public money in payment to agents to collect children. Mr. Seton, who has been a faithful agent of the So-

53

ciety, made that fact known, and stated that by this means 800 children were collected. And to whom was this money given? To Tract Distributors—a very good occupation theirs, I have no doubt—but at the same time that was rather a singular appropriation by men so extremely scrupulous lest any portion of the public money should go to the support of any sect. But I suppose that was on the principle of what Mr. Ketchum calls "giving and taking," that is, you give a tract and take a child! (laughter and cheers.)

Then we have quite an effort on the part of Mr. Ketchum, to prove that the Trustees discharge their onerous duties much better than officers elected by the people. I will quote his remarks on that point.

"This Public School Society receives its daily sustenance from the representatives of the people—and the moment that sustenance is withdrawn, it dies—it cannot carry on its operations for a day."

A most beautiful subversion of the actual order! For so far from the Common Council patronizing the Society, it is the Society that patronizes the Common Council—taking them into partnership the moment they are elected, and so far from being dependent on the Council, as was well remarked by a greater authority than I am on this subject, the Council are dependent on the Society. The schools belong to the Society, just as much as the Harlaem bridge does to the Company who built it. What remedy is there then. The Society, self constituted a close corporation, takes into partnership the Common Council, which then becomes part and parcel—bone of the bone, and flesh of the flesh—of the Society; and if any difference arises between the citizens and the Society, a committee of that very Society adjudicates in the cause! Thus we have found, that the Common Council after having denied our claim, and even when about to retire and give place to their successors, followed us to Albany; and their last act—like that of the retreating Parthian who flung his dart behind him—was to lay *their* remonstrance on the table of the tribunal to which we had appealed. Mr. Ketchum says:—

"Here are agents of the people—men who, having a desire to serve mankind, associate together, they offer to take the superintendence of particular works, they offer themselves to the public as agents to carry out certain benevolent purposes and, instead of paying men for the labor, they volunteer to do it for you, "without money and without price," under your directions—to do it as your servants—and to give an account to you and an account to the Legislature. Voluntary public service is always more efficient than labor done by servants chosen in any other way."

So that because they serve gratuitously they discharge their duties much better than if elected by the people! Well, let us improve upon the hint. Perhaps some of them may be kind enough to discharge the more important functions of the government for nothing!. But if volunteers be more efficient than officers chosen by the votes of the people, let us abolish the farce of elections altogether. Not satisfied with this, Mr. Ketchum also, would seem to contend, that the volunteers ought not to be held responsible!

To establish his views on this point, Mr. Ketchum refers to charitable and benevolent Institutions. But where is the justice of the comparison! The sick are incompetent to secure their own protection and recovery. The inmates of the House of Refuge, on which Mr. Ketchum has a beautiful apostrophe, referring to his own share in the erection of that one established in this city, are likewise unable to take care of themselves. And here let me say, in all sincerity to Mr. Ketchum, that if he and the Public School Society determine to perpetuate their system; if they continue to exclude religion from education, and at the same time deprive four-fifths of the children, as now, of any education at all; then he had better stretch his lines and lay the foundations of Houses of Refuge, as the appropriate supplement to the system. Neither does the comparison hold, as I have before shown, in reference to Lunatic Asylums, &c. &c.

Then Mr. Ketchum goes on to illustrate farther, and says:—

‘ But it is said, and said too in the report of the Secretary, that he proposes to retain these Public Schools. How retain them? One of the features of the proposed new law is, that all school monies shall be paid to the teachers. Under such a law we cannot live a day—no, a day."

What an acknowledgment is that! That a law, which would make education free—giving equal rights to all—would be the death-warrant of the Public School Society!

There is another point on which Mr. Ketchum does not now dwell so emphatically. He says that there were a large number of tax-payers who—wonderful to relate!—asked for the privilege of being taxed; asked for that privilege for the purpose of supplying the Public School Society with money to carry out their benevolent purposes. Mr. Ketchum seems to consider that at that time there was a kind of covenant made between these petitioners to be taxed, and the State authorities; that when they petitioned and were taxed, the authorities of the State bound themselves to keep up this system *in perpetuum*. But did these persons ask to be taxed exclusively out of their own pockets, or did they ask for a system of taxation which should reach ALL the tax paying citizens of New-York! There is a fallacy in Mr. Ketchum's argument here. He supposes that because these persons are large property holders, that they are therefore, *par excellence*, the payers of taxes. He forgets that it is a fact well understood in the science of political economy, that the consumer is, after all, the tax-payer; that it is the tenants occupying the property of those rich men, and returning them their large rents, who are actually the tax payers. And what peculiar merit, then, can Mr. Ketchum claim for these owners of property, and petitioners to have all the rest of the citizens taxed as well as themselves! But he insists there was an agreement—a covenant entered into between them, and the State authorities, and if you interfere with its provisions, you must release these tax-payers from their obligations as such. With all my heart, I have no objection! All we want is that there should be no unjust interference; no exclusive system; no extraneous authority interposed between the tax-payer and the purpose for which the tax is collected. But the fact that others, besides these petitioners, are equally involved in the burthen, demolishes this argument of Mr. Ketchum.

In his conclusion the learned gentleman insists, that unless the

Society remain as it is, it cannot exist. And then goes on further, for it would be impossible for him to close his speech without again reminding the Senate that we are Roman Catholics. He says:—

" The people in New York understand the subject, and the Roman Catholics cannot say that they will not be heard as well there as here   Why not leave the matter to us, 'the people of the city of New York ?"

Thus Mr. Ketchum, after having first endeavored to impress the minds of the Senate, that we had had all imaginable fair play; that other denominations had made applications similar to ours—which is not the fact;—that our petition had uniformly been denied in the several Boards representing the people of New-York—whereas he knew that in this question the people of New-York was never even represented by the Common Council;—he goes on to say at last: "Why not leave the matter to us—the people of the city of New-York?" I trust not, if a committee of the Public School Society, called the Common Council, are to be at once parties and judges. I hope that the question will not be referred back, although for Mr. Ketchum's satisfaction, I may state, that if it were so referred, the Common Council would not, I will venture to say, now decide upon it by such a vote as they did before, when one man alone had the courage—whether he was right or wrong—to say nay, when all said yes! (Loud and long continued cheering.) In consequence of that vote—as they have since taken care to tell us—this gentleman lost his election; but, what was of infinitely greater importance, he preserved his honor. (Renewed applause.) Were the matter now before the Common Council, they would see a thousand and one reasons for hesitation before deciding as before. For when public men see that any measure is likely to be popular, they can find abundant reasons for taking a favorable view of the question. I will refer Mr. Ketchum to a sign from which he may learn what he pleases. Since the Common Council that denied our claims went out of office, their successors have had the matter before them; and when in the Board of Assistants it was proposed to pass a resolution, requesting the Legislature to defer the consideration of the question, the motion *was negatived by a tie vote.*

Still Mr. Ketchum will have the end of this speech something like the end of the last.   Then he said that this was a most distressing topic to the gentlemen of the Public School Society —that they were men of peace—that I do not controvert, but certainly I must say, that in the course of this contest, they appear to have exhibited a spirit contrary to their natures!—but so peaceful were they, Mr. Ketchum said, that, if any longer annoyed, they would throw up their office and retire! (cheers aud laughter.)   But after all, they could send their agents to Albany to oppose us there—the one, Dr. Rockwell, to disseminate a burlesque on our faith, from Tristram Shandy—the other, Mr. Ketchum, to plead as zealously, but I think not as successfully against the recognition of our claims.   Mr. Ketchum says—

" Now the contest is renewed, and the trustees engage in it with extreme reluctance , they have no personal interests to advance, and they are very unwilling to be put in hostile array against any of their fellow citizens."

Mr. Chairman—The lateness of the hour admonishes me that

I have trespassed too much upon your patience. I have but one observation to make in conclusion.

These gentlemen have spoken much, and laid great emphasis on the importance of morality, but as I have already remarked, morality is not always judged of by the same criterion. Let me illustrate this. According to the morality which *my* religion teaches, if I rob a man, or injure him in his property, and desire to be reconciled to God, I must, *first of all*, if it be in my power, make reparation to the man whom I have injured. Again, if I should unfortunately rob my neighbor of his good name; of his reputation; either by accident or through malice, before I can hope for reconciliation with an offended God, I must repair the injury and restore my neighbor's good name. If I belied him, I must acknowledge the lie as publicly as it was uttered—*that* is Catholic morality. Well now, these gentlemen have belied us—they have put forward and circulated a document which existed only in the imagination of Sterne—a foul document—*and represented it as a part of our creed.* I do not say that they directly required this to be done; but their Agent did it, and he cannot deny it. I wonder now, then, if they will have such a sense of *morality* as will impel them to endeavor to repair the injury thus done to our reputation by any official declaration that that is a spurious document? I wonder if the conscientious morality that presides over the "Journal of Commerce" will prompt its editors to such a course? If it do not, then it is a morality different from ours.

I apprehend that no such reparation will be offered for the injury we have sustained by the everlasting harangue of abuse and virtuperation that has been poured out against us for these few years past. Have we not been assailed with a foul and infamous fiction, in the pages of a work called "Maria Monk?" and have its Reverend authors ever stood forward to do us justice, and acknowledge the untruth which, knowing it to be so, they published? Have they ever attempted to counteract that obscene poison which they disseminated, corrupting the morals of youth throughout every hamlet in the land! Whilst denouncing in their ecclesiastical assemblies, the works of Byron and Bulwer, did they include in their denunciations, the filthy and enormous lie, published under their auspices, the writings of "Maria Monk?"

What idea then must we form of their morality and religion? And here it would be unjust to omit mentioning that many Protestants, not under the influence of blinded bigotry, have done us justice on this point. In particular, I refer to the conduct of one distinguished Protestant writer who cannot be accused of great partiality for us, but who exposed and refuted authors and abettors of this filthy libel to which I have referred. I know that it would be incorrect and unjust, to say that thousands of others, sincere Protestants, but high minded honorable men, have not taken the same view of the subject. But I speak particularly of the morality of the authors and publishers of these abominable slanders, and I regret that the Public School Society, by their recent proceedings, should have allowed themselves to sink to a kindred degradation! (The Rt. Rev. Prelate, here resumed his seat amid thunders of applause, which lasted several minutes.)

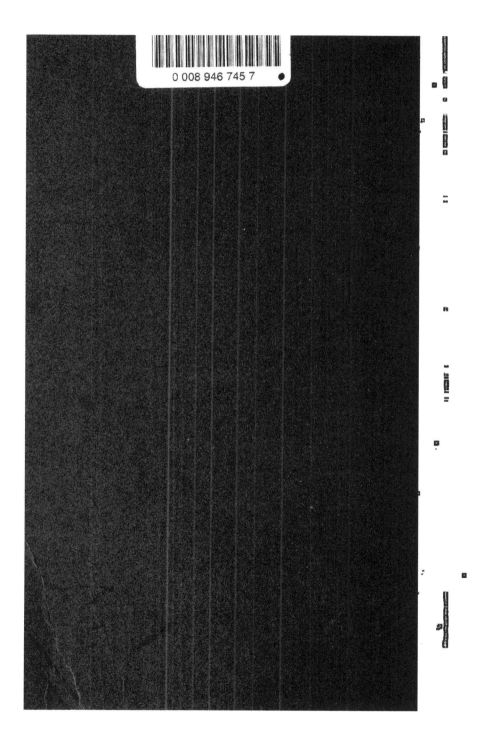

0 008 946 745 7

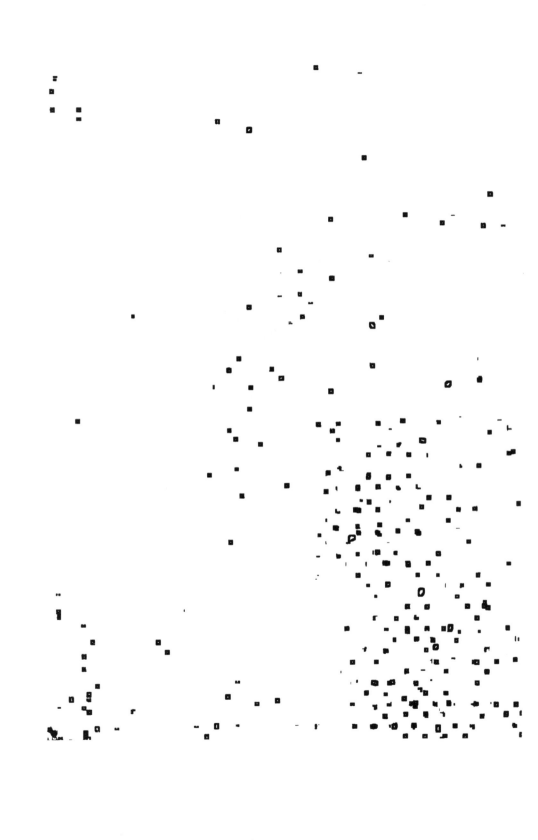

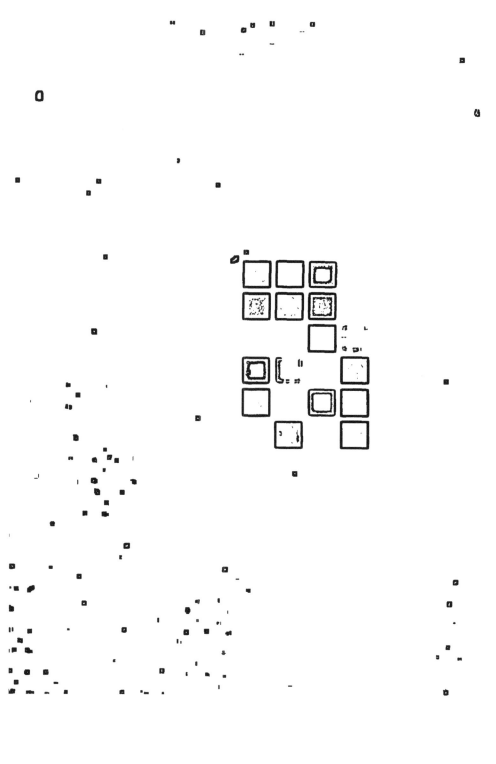

Lightning Source UK Ltd.
Milton Keynes UK
UKHW020646110321
380169UK00006B/621